All's Fair

CW00420399

A play

Frank Vickery

Samuel French – London
New York – Sydney – Toronto – Hollywood

© 1988 BY FRANK VICKERY

Rights of Performance by Amateurs are controlled by Samuel French Ltd, 52 Fitzroy Street, London W1T 5JR, and they, or their authorized agents, issue licences to amateurs on payment of a fee. **It is an infringement of the Copyright to give any performance or public reading of the play before the fee has been paid and the licence issued.**

The Royalty Fee indicated below is subject to contract and subject to variation at the sole discretion of Samuel French Ltd.

Basic fee for each and every
performance by amateurs   Code L
in the British Isles

The publication of this play does not imply that it is necessarily available for performance by amateurs or professionals, either in the British Isles or Overseas. Amateurs and professionals considering a production are strongly advised in their own interests to apply to the appropriate agents for written consent before starting rehearsals or booking a theatre or hall.

ISBN 0 573 01675 5

Please see page iv for further copyright information

ALL'S FAIR

First performed by the Spectacle Theatre Company, at the YMCA Theatre, Swansea, on 16th October, 1983, with the following cast of characters:

Dilys	Terri O'Donoghue
Sophie	Lynne Hunter
Brenda	Rosamonde Hutt
Mother	Veda Warwick
Trevor	Simon Bent
Greg	Richard Locke

Directed by Joan Mills

*

It was subsequently performed by the Parc and Dare Theatre Company at the Maytime International Festival of Theatre in Dundalk, Northern Ireland, with the following cast of characters:

Dilys	Lynfa Williams
Sophie	Pam Gould
Brenda	Elaine Andrews
Mother	Iris Griffiths
Trevor	Kelvin Lawrence-Jones
Greg	Brian Meadows

Directed by Brian Meadows

COPYRIGHT INFORMATION

(See also page ii)

This play is fully protected under the Copyright Laws of the British Commonwealth of Nations, the United States of America and all countries of the Berne and Universal Copyright Conventions.

All rights including Stage, Motion Picture, Radio, Television, Public Reading, and Translation into Foreign Languages, are strictly reserved.

No part of this publication may lawfully be reproduced in ANY form or by any means — photocopying, typescript, recording (including video-recording), manuscript, electronic, mechanical, or otherwise—or be transmitted or stored in a retrieval system, without prior permission.

Licences for amateur performances are issued subject to the understanding that it shall be made clear in all advertising matter that the audience will witness an amateur performance; that the names of the authors of the plays shall be included on all programmes; and that the integrity of the authors' work will be preserved.

The Royalty Fee is subject to contract and subject to variation at the sole discretion of Samuel French Ltd.

In Theatres or Halls seating Four Hundred or more the fee will be subject to negotiation.

In Territories Overseas the fee quoted above may not apply. A fee will be quoted on application to our local authorized agent, or if there is no such agent, on application to Samuel French Ltd, London.

VIDEO-RECORDING OF AMATEUR PRODUCTIONS

Please note that the copyright laws governing video-recording are extremely complex and that it should not be assumed that any play may be video-recorded for whatever purpose without first obtaining the permission of the appropriate agents. The fact that a play is published by Samuel French Ltd does not indicate that video rights are available or that Samuel French Ltd controls such rights.

CHARACTERS

Dilys
Brenda
Sophie
Mother
Trevor
Greg

The action of the play takes place in the living-room of the family's house somewhere in Wales

ACT I SCENE 1 Late one Friday evening in May
SCENE 2 Early August. Afternoon

ACT II SCENE 1 And hour or so later
SCENE 2 Late August. Afternoon
SCENE 3 September. Evening

Time—1942

Other plays by Frank Vickery, published by Samuel French

After I'm Gone
A Night on the Tiles
A Night Out
One O'Clock from the House

ACT I

The living-room of the family home. Late one Friday evening in May, 1942

When the play opens, Brenda is sitting on the settee. She is a girl of fourteen. We only see her from the orange glow of the fire as the lights in the room are off

After a moment or so the front door opens and closes and we hear two voices from the passage. The door to the living-room is opened and Dilys enters followed by Sophie. They are clippies with the local transport company and have just finished an afternoon shift. They are in uniform

Dilys Ooooh it's all in darkness. Switch the lights on, Soph.
Sophie Which one is it?
Dilys The middle one.
Sophie (*trying the light switch*) The shilling's gone.
Dilys (*going into the hall*) Hang on, I'll see if there's one under the runner. Here's one. Wait a minute, you'll need a chair. (*She hands Sophie a chair*)

Sophie climbs up to put the shilling in the meter. As the Lights come on, Dilys screams seeing Brenda

Sophie What is it?
Brenda It's only me.
Dilys What are you doing sitting in the dark?
Brenda I like it sometimes.
Dilys (*drawing the curtains*) Where is everyone?
Brenda Trevor's gone down the *King's Head* and Mammy hasn't come back yet.
Dilys I thought you were going to the pictures with her?
Brenda No. I got ready too. Had my bath and everything ... but then I changed my mind. Mammy went with Mrs Condon instead.
Dilys She's late coming back.
Brenda She said she'd call in and get some chips for supper.
Dilys Still, she should be back by now. Take your coat off, Soph.
Sophie (*doing so*) I wish I'd gone home and changed.
Dilys Don't be silly, he knows you're a clippy. I've told him you're on the same shift as me.
Sophie I'd feel better if I didn't have my uniform on.
Brenda Have you come round to see our Trevor?
Dilys Put the kettle on, Brend, there's a luv. (*To Sophie*) Give it to me.

She takes Sophie's coat and hangs it with her own in the passage

Brenda (*after giving Sophie a good look over*) He's not interested.
Sophie (*looking at Brenda suspiciously*) Who?
Brenda Trevor.
Sophie In what?
Brenda You.
Sophie What makes you say that?
Brenda I know him.
Sophie Well you can't know him very well, because Dilys told me he keeps a photo of me pinned up in his bedroom.
Brenda (*wickedly*) I bet she didn't tell you where he's pinned it.
Sophie (*thinking about it*) No. I don't believe she did.

Dilys enters

Dilys Did you see to the kettle, Brend?
Brenda Just going.

She exits to the kitchen smiling smugly at Sophie as she goes

Sophie Is she having me on or what?
Dilys What did she say?
Sophie You weren't pulling my leg when you said that Trevor keeps a photo of me pinned up in his bedroom, were you?
Dilys Of course not. Look, he likes you.
Sophie Tell me where then.
Dilys Where what?
Sophie He's pinned it. Tell me where he's pinned it.
Dilys (*after a slight pause*) I don't think I remember.
Sophie On the wall?

Dilys shakes her head

What about the ceiling? What's-his-name did that, didn't he, in that film. You know, we saw it in the Palace a couple of months ago. He pinned her photograph on the ceiling so's that her face would be the last thing he'd see at night, and the first thing he'd see in the morning. I think that's awful romantic. I wish you'd tell me where it is.

Brenda enters

Brenda I'll tell you. It's behind the bedroom door.
Sophie (*a little disappointed*) You're sure it's not on the ceiling?
Brenda (*shaking her head*) Behind the bedroom door. Smack right in the middle of his dart-board.
Sophie (*laughing*) You're having me on. (*She continues to laugh then stops suddenly*) She is, isn't she? She is having me on?
Dilys (*trying to cover up*) Of course she is. (*She gives Brenda a look*) That's not Sophie, Brend. That's Betty Grable.

They all laugh except Brenda

Sophie Fancy mistaking me for Betty Grable. (*To Dilys*) Hey, did I tell you

I had a fella on the top deck the night before last swore blind I was Gracie Fields. I told him I wasn't but I had to sing four bars of "Sally" before he'd believe me. I reckon it was all a decoy though. You know, take your mind off collecting the fare. He'd have got away with it too if I hadn't seen him trying to slip the money back into his pocket. Some men are crafty, aren't they?

Brenda Trevor's not.

Sophie Some men I said.

Dilys I'm surprised you don't know him, Soph.

Sophie Oh I do a bit. Well not to talk to. I could pick him out in a crowd like. Seen him on the bus once or twice. But I don't know him to talk to— not to have a conversation.

Dilys He's a nice boy.

Sophie So you keep saying.

Dilys He's just your type Soph, honest. He's not a womanizer. Very quietly spoken. A bit fussy with his food but taking everything into consideration you're dead right for each other.

Sophie I hope so. It's ever so embarrassing when you haven't got a fella.

Dilys Yeah.

Sophie What do you mean, "yeah"? You wouldn't know.

Dilys I would.

Sophie What about that American then?

Dilys makes a face, not wanting her to say too much in front of Brenda

I don't know what you see in them they're all chocolates and chewing gum. What did Trevor say when you asked him if he wanted to take me home?

There is a pause

You did ask him, didn't you?

Dilys Of course I did.

Sophie You're looking very sheepish, Dilys. Come on, tell me.

Brenda I'll tell you.

Sophie (*to Dilys*) She's a hell of a girl, isn't she?

Brenda Go on, Dil, tell her.

Dilys (*scornfully*) Brenda!

Brenda He said, "If you bring that——"

Dilys Go and see to the kettle, Brenda, before it boils away.

Sophie Let her finish first.

Brenda is about to open her mouth

Dilys Brenda!

Brenda returns to the kitchen

Sophie (*after a slight pause*) You've gone and put me right in it you have, haven't you?

Dilys It'll be all right, don't worry.

Sophie I can imagine his face when he walks in and sees me sitting here.

Dilys If he didn't like you why would he keep your photo in his bedroom?
Sophie I don't believe he's got my photo. I bet it's somebody who looks like
  me.
Dilys Somebody like Rita Hayworth or Lana Turner.
Sophie Or Gracie bloody Fields. Tell me what he said, Dilys, or I'm going
  home.
Dilys If I told you what he said you'd go home anyway.
Sophie Right. Well that's it. I'm off.
Dilys No. Wait a minute, Soph.
Sophie Where did you put my coat?
Dilys You don't understand. Look—let me explain. (*After a slight pause*)
  Our Trevor never goes looking for anything. You've always got to find it
  for him and put it right under his nose. Do you know what I mean?

Sophie shrugs

He might not think much of you now but he will. Given time.
Sophie Time is what I haven't got.
Dilys Give it a try that's all I'm asking. If it doesn't work out—well that's
  that. What's the harm done.
Sophie (*pausing as she pats her hair*) Oh OK. Sure I look all right?
Dilys You look lovely.

The front door slams

Sophie (*panicking*) Is that him?
Dilys I don't know.
Sophie Where shall I sit?
Dilys Stay where you are.
Sophie I want to go and freshen up.
Dilys It's too late.

Mother enters rather quickly carrying a parcel of chips

Mother (*handing them to Dilys as she passes*) Here you, quick, take these.
  (*She goes to the kitchen raising her voice as she goes*) I've got to go to the
  toilet. Sort them out, Dilys, there's plenty there.

She exits. The back door slams

Dilys Fancy chips, Soph?
Sophie I've got to watch my figure.
Dilys All right, you can watch it go fat.
Sophie I'll just have a couple on a plate.
Dilys (*calling*) Bring some plates in, Brend.
Sophie I panicked a bit then.
Dilys He'll be here in a minute now. (*Calling again*) And the salt and
  vinegar.
Sophie Got any fresh bread? I'll make a sandwich.
Dilys I'll get some.

Dilys exits to the kitchen as Brenda enters carrying three plates. She stands for a moment looking at Sophie; when she is happy that she has Sophie's attention, she speaks

Brenda He said, "If you bring that fat-arsed——"
Sophie Is that what he called me?
Brenda (*nodding*) He said, "If you bring that fat-arsed midget in this house, I'll break wind the entire time she's here."
Sophie I thought he was a quiet boy.
Brenda Don't you believe it.
Sophie (*after a slight pause*) He wouldn't do that, would he?
Brenda What?
Sophie Break wind all night.
Brenda Wait and see.
Sophie I don't think I'll bother. Where's my coat?

Dilys enters with a loaf of bread

Dilys How many pieces, Soph?
Sophie Forget it—I'm going home.
Dilys I thought it was all settled.
Sophie I can't stand anyone who breaks wind.
Dilys What are you talking about?
Brenda I'll go and wet the tea.

She exits to the kitchen

Sophie I haven't spoken to my grandfather for two years because he did it once when we were all having supper.
Dilys What's going on?
Sophie Brenda told me what Trevor said.
Dilys (*after a slight pause*) Oh.
Sophie He did say it then?
Dilys He didn't mean it. Was it one piece you said?
Sophie I'll have two.
Dilys What about your figure?
Sophie To hell with it. (*After a slight pause*) He won't then?
Dilys (*cutting the bread*) What?
Sophie Break wind?
Dilys Don't be silly.
Sophie Are you sure? Because if he did my stomach would never stick it.
Dilys Neither would mine.
Sophie It's not a very nice subject to be talking about.
Dilys It doesn't go with chips, does it?
Sophie Let's talk about something else.
Dilys All right.
Sophie Where's your mother?
Dilys Out the toilet.

They both laugh

Sophie We can't seem to get away from it. Hey, my mother had a letter from my father last week.

Dilys I didn't know he'd been called up?
Sophie Oh yeah. He gets called regularly, to the *Royal Oak*. He went down
  there last March and we haven't seen him since. My mother's expecting a
  letter any day saying "Missing presumed drunk". (*She laughs*) He'll come
  back one day! When he's sober.
Dilys Where does he go?
Sophie His sister's.

Brenda enters with the teapot

Dilys Bring the cups in as well, Brend.

Brenda puts the teapot down and returns to the kitchen

Sophie Is she always like that?
Dilys Like what?
Sophie Well I don't know. She seems a bit strange to me.
Dilys It's her age.
Sophie How old is she?
Dilys Just gone fourteen.
Sophie (*smiling as she reminisces*) Do you remember when you were
  fourteen?
Dilys No.
Sophie (*sighing*) No nor me.
Dilys Of course I remember it. It was only a couple of years ago.
Sophie For you, yes. It was fourteen years ago for me.
Dilys Is it twenty-eight you are then?
Sophie Twenty-nine coming up.
Dilys I want to be married before I'm twenty-five.
Sophie So did I. It was my dream. Now all I dream about is being married
  before I'm thirty.

Brenda enters with cups

Dilys Thanks, luv. You've only brought three plates in, Brend.
Brenda That's right.
Dilys But we're four.
Brenda I don't want any.
Dilys Why's that?
Brenda I'm not hungry.
Dilys Are you all right?
Sophie I said she looked a bit funny.
Dilys You look off-colour.
Brenda Stop fussing. I just don't want any supper that's all.

Mother calls from the outside toilet

Mother (*off*) Brenda?

Brenda goes off towards the kitchen

  (*Off*) Brenda?
Brenda (*off*) What do you want?

Mother (*off*) Fetch some paper out.
Sophie Fancy sitting in the dark.
Dilys There's something up.

Brenda enters

Brenda Where's the paper?
Dilys Under the cushion.

Brenda picks up the cushion of the settee and takes the newspaper. Dilys watches her

Is that what she wants?
Brenda Yes.
Dilys Don't give her that. There's some orange papers in the sideboard drawer.

Brenda throws the newspaper on to the settee then takes the orange papers from the sideboard

Brenda Will two be enough?
Mother (*off*) Brenda?
Dilys Tell her to stretch it.

Brenda goes

Sophie You save them as well, do you?
Dilys Anything's better than this. (*She shows her the newspaper before she puts it back under the cushion*)
Sophie I wish I'd brought my compact with me.
Dilys You look all right.
Sophie I don't want to look all right—I want to look beautiful. I'm dying for a cup of tea.
Dilys I'm just pouring it.
Sophie You can't lend me one, can you?
Dilys What?
Sophie A compact.
Dilys There's one in my bag on the sideboard.

Sophie takes out the compact and returns to her seat before opening it

Sophie The glass is cracked.
Dilys I know.
Sophie It was like that before I looked at it mind.
Dilys (*laughing*) I said I know.
Sophie Lovely smell. (*Powdering her face*) There's a lovely smell on this powder.
Dilys How many sugars?
Sophie One.

Brenda enters

I've got to be careful.
Brenda She's watching her weight.

Dilys Well it's all ready.
Sophie (*looking closer in the mirror*) I'm sure I've got a boil coming.
Dilys Do you want to come to the table?
Sophie I'll have mine by here if it's all right.

Dilys hands her a plate of chips, two slices of bread, and a cup of tea

Dilys Put it on the arm, it's what we usually do.

Sophie puts the tea down on the arm of the chair and rests the plate on her lap

Sure you won't have any, Brend?
Brenda No.
Sophie I love chip sandwiches.
Dilys Do you want more salt and vinegar?
Sophie No, I'm all right I think. (*Still looking in the mirror*) You cut bread nice and thin, Dil. When I make a sandwich it's like a door step. (*She laughs*)
Dilys (*after a slight pause*) Why don't you go to bed, Brend?
Brenda I'm not ready yet.
Dilys You look all in.
Sophie She's not the only one. I wish I could get rid of these bags. (*She closes the compact*) There that'll have to do. (*She holds up the compact*) What shall I do with this?

Dilys takes the compact from her and puts it back in her bag. The back door opens and closes and Mother speaks from the kitchen

Mother (*off*) Have you seen to the chips, Dilys?
Dilys It's all ready, yes.
Mother (*off*) I haven't been taken short like that for a long time. I can usually time it pretty well. Good job we didn't move to that house in Phillips Terrace or I'd have never made it.

She enters from the kitchen wiping her hands in a towel

Dilys Mam, this is my friend, Sophie.
Mother (*hitting Dilys with the towel*) Why didn't you tell me we had visitors? Letting me carry on like that. Hello, luv. What did you say your name was?
Sophie Sophie.
Mother Sophie what?
Sophie Hepton.
Mother Whose girl are you then?
Dilys They haven't been here long.
Mother Oooh Dilys, doesn't she look like that singer, you know, the one in the films.
Sophie (*singing*) "Sally, Sally——"
Mother Vera Lynn.
Sophie (*still singing*) "There'll be blue birds over——"
Mother I can't get over it. You're her spitting image.
Dilys Have your chips, Mam, or they will get cold.

Mother (*sitting at the table*) You work with our Dilys then, do you?
Sophie We're on the same shift, yes.
Mother Like it?
Sophie It's a job.
Mother Of course it is. Our Dilys loves it, don't you?
Dilys Well it was either that or the arsenal.
Sophie I had a cousin working at the arsenal.
Mother Had?

Sophie nods then makes a gesture with her hands at the same time making an exploding noise from the back of her throat

She had an accident?
Sophie She blew up the canteen.
Mother Oh there's sad.
Sophie Yes. They had to bring sandwiches in for a month.
Mother You've got to be careful in them places.
Sophie It's too late for her to be careful now.
Mother Oh, I see.
Sophie The head cook resigned after that.
Mother There's childish.
Sophie All because it ruined his bread and butter pudding.
Mother Well it would.
Sophie It was still in one piece though. All covered in mortar in the middle of the ceiling. The Army came and took it away. They said they wanted to analyse it because it was the only thing that survived the blast. They said they might be able to line the tanks with it or something.
Brenda Trevor's late.
Mother What time is it?
Dilys Ten to eleven.
Mother He'll be here now. (*To Sophie*) You haven't met our Trevor, have you?
Sophie Not yet.
Mother Nice boy.
Sophie Dilys was saying.
Mother He's awful good to me. Well, and to the girls. He's older than Dilys. He's twenty-seven.
Sophie That's a nice age.
Brenda For what?
Sophie (*pausing slightly as she gives Brenda a look*) For staying out late.
Dilys I thought that seeing as it was a bit late, he'd walk Sophie home.
Mother Oh I expect he will.
Dilys I'd walk her home myself but I'd only have to walk all the way back home on my own.
Mother Trevor'll do it.
Sophie (*coming to the end of her sandwich*) You're sure he won't mind? I'd hate to put him out or anything.

No-one answers. The front door slams

Is that him?

Before anyone can answer, Trevor stands in the doorway. He claps his hands together and rubs them, smiling

Trevor Thought I could smell chips.
Mother You're too late, boy, they've all gone.
Trevor Didn't you keep any?
Brenda (*pointing at Sophie*) *She* had yours, Trev.

Trevor looks at Sophie

Dilys Trevor, this is my friend, Sophie.
Sophie Hello Trevor, pleased to meet you.
Trevor Sophie?
Sophie Yes, you know that fat-arsed midget.

They both laugh

Trevor Oh Sophie, yes of course. You're fatter than your photo.
Sophie (*pleased*) You have got one then?
Trevor Oh ay. It's full of holes now though.
Sophie Dilys told me you were shy.
Trevor Did she?
Sophie On the quiet side she said.
Trevor Yes well she would say that, wouldn't she.
Sophie Why?
Trevor Try and make me sound attractive. She wants to marry me off.
Sophie What for?
Trevor She wants my bedroom.
Sophie You don't seem a bit quiet to me.
Trevor Oh I am. Aren't I, Mother?
Mother What?
Trevor Quiet.
Mother Ay, when you're sleeping.
Trevor Well it was nice meeting you, Sandra.
Sophie Sophie.
Trevor Sorry.

He winks at Brenda and she giggles

You'll have to excuse me now, I'm going to have a bit of supper.
Mother Come and have your chips.
Trevor I thought I didn't have any.
Mother You know what thought done.

Mother goes out to the kitchen

Trevor takes off his jacket and puts it on the back of a chair. He then sits at the table

Dilys (*cutting bread*) How many pieces?
Trevor One.
Brenda She wants to know if you'll take her home, Trev.
Trevor Who?

Brenda Sophie.
Dilys (*scornfully*) Brenda!
Sophie Don't listen to her. I don't mind walking home on my own.
Brenda It's all arranged. They've been waiting for you to come in.
Sophie (*embarrassed*) Dilys asked me to come in for some supper, that's all.
Brenda She's lying Trev.
Dilys (*to Brenda*) I'll want to speak to you after.
Sophie You shouldn't say things like that, Brenda. You're putting your
brother on a spot.
Brenda I'm not putting him on a spot.
Sophie Yes you are. She is, isn't she, Dilys?
Dilys (*to Sophie*) Take no notice.
Sophie What would your brother want to take me home for anyway? (*Slight
pause*) I mean, he could take home who he wanted. (*Slight pause*) He
wouldn't be interested in me. (*Slight pause*) And I'm used to walking
home on my own anyway. With a figure like mine I've had to get used to
that. No. Trevor wouldn't be interested in me. (*She waits for some sort of
contradiction from Trevor but one doesn't come*) Fetch my coat, Dil? (*She
tries to hide her embarrassment*)

Dilys goes out to the hall to get Sophie's coat, then comes back

As Sophie receives her coat, she realizes that Dilys has brought hers too

Oh there's no need for you to come, honest.
Dilys I want to.
Sophie No, don't be soft.
Dilys You can't go on your own.
Sophie Dil? (*She puts her hand on Dilys's arm*) I'd rather be by myself.

*Dilys watches her as she puts on her coat. She has trouble with it so Dilys helps
her*

Good-night then.
Dilys (*quietly*) Sorry, Soph.

Mother enters from the kitchen with chips

Mother Here you are, Trevor.
Trevor Wait a minute. (*He puts his jacket back on*)
Mother Where are you going?
Trevor I'm taking the dog for a walk. (*He winks at his mother*)
Mother What about your supper?
Trevor I'll have it when I get back.

*He opens the passage door and holds it open for Sophie to exit. Before she
does however, she beams at everyone. As she turns and glides out of the
room she sticks her tongue out at Brenda. Trevor closes the curtain behind
them*

Mother Well I never expected that.

She takes the chips out to the kitchen then returns during the next

Dilys (*smiling*) It's surprising what he'll do if you don't ask him.
Brenda You can't wait to get him out of that bedroom, can you?
Dilys I *should* have a room of my own. Anyway, I don't know what you're moaning about, if I did have a bedroom of my own so would you.
Brenda It's not so important to me.
Dilys It will be when you're my age.
Mother I hope you two are not going to start.
Dilys It's her fault. She's been funny since I came in.
Brenda There's nothing wrong with me.
Dilys Even Sophie said about it.
Brenda She should talk.
Mother (*to Dilys*) She's a bit of a girl.
Brenda She's not all there.
Dilys There's nothing wrong with her.
Mother A bit highly strung she is.
Brenda Strung she ought to be, from the ceiling.
Mother That's enough from you. Go to bed.
Brenda No not yet.
Mother Now!
Brenda I'm not ready.
Mother Go up, go on. I'll be straight behind you.
Brenda Can't I say a bit longer?
Mother No.
Brenda Please?
Mother (*opening the passage curtain*) Up the stairs.

Reluctantly Brenda leaves the room

Brenda Night, Dil.

She exits

Dilys Night.
Mother (*closing the door*) There's another one who doesn't listen to me.
Dilys It's her age.
Mother And what's your excuse?

Dilys doesn't answer

(*Sitting down*) Oh, I'm dead beat.
Dilys Why don't you go straight up then?
Mother Yes I will when I'm ready. Sit down.
Dilys I was just going to clear away the dishes.
Mother You can do them after. Sit down.
Dilys I'd rather do them——
Mother (*firmly*) Dilys! Sit down.
Dilys Oh I see.
Mother Do you?
Dilys I'm going to have another talking to. (*After a slight pause*) Do you want another cup of tea?
Mother No. (*After a slight pause*) I was talking to Mrs Condon tonight.

Dilys I thought that was a bit obvious seeing as you went to the pictures with her.

Mother I don't want any lip. (*After a slight pause*) She told me he was married.

Dilys Who?

Mother You know who I'm talking about. That American.

Dilys (*after a slight pause*) I think I'll have another one. (*She goes to the table and pours*)

Mother Is it right?

Dilys (*quietly*) Yes.

Mother And you still bother with him?

Dilys It's too late to stop.

Mother You're a silly girl, Dilys. I suppose he's promised to leave his wife?

Dilys He hasn't promised anything.

Mother I don't know what your father would say if he were still alive.

Dilys Don't you? I do. He'd say, "Grab it, luv. Grab it and hang on to it as long as it makes you happy."

Mother just stares, deep in thought

And he does, Mam. I am happy.

Mother Be careful.

Dilys I'll be all right.

Mother He'll say things he doesn't mean.

Dilys He's not a liar.

Mother No maybe not—but he's lonely. And when you're lonely you'll say lots of things. You mean them at the time, but there's a war on, people act differently in times like these.

Dilys I thought about it. About getting involved. I didn't rush into it. I took my time. The trouble was I took so long to decide by the time I'd made up my mind it was too late anyway. I was past the point of no return. (*After a slight pause*) I wish you wouldn't worry though.

Mother How can I not worry?

Dilys I'm twenty-two.

Mother What difference does that make? Let me tell you, Dilys—I don't think you ever stop worrying about your kids, not even when you're dead and in your grave. You won't believe that of course, not until you get married and have kids of your own. And I hope you took notice of the order I said that.

Dilys What?

Mother I said get married and have children.

Dilys (*a little embarrassed*) Oh Mam!

Mother It's so easy to give in. I'm telling you this because if I was thirty years younger and single I'd . . . (*She stops speaking and grimaces in pain*)

Dilys Mam, what's the matter?

Mother It's all right.

Dilys What is it?

Mother It'll go now. It doesn't last.

Dilys Have you seen the doctor?

Mother It's colic, that's all.
Dilys Does Trevor know?

Dilys and her mother stare at each other for a moment

Mother What?
Dilys (*still staring*) That you're ill.
Mother No. And don't you go telling him either.
Dilys Why?
Mother Because he'll worry.
Dilys I'll worry too.
Mother (*still in pain*) Don't say anything, Dil, will you?
Dilys (*after a slight pause*) Is it serious?
Mother Don't ask me.
Dilys Why?
Mother Because I've never been any good at pretending.
Dilys (*about to cry*) Oh Mam.
Mother Don't er . . . (*Almost crying herself*) Don't get upset. You mustn't.
We mustn't show the others. There, it's going now.
Dilys Do you know what it is?
Mother (*after a slight pause*) No.
Dilys You're right. You aren't very good at pretending.

Brenda enters and goes straight to the kitchen. As she does so:

Brenda I want a cup of water.

She exits to the kitchen

Mother I'm going up to bed. Wash and wipe the dishes will you? And don't
be long behind me.
Dilys Don't go to bed yet. Stay here and talk to me.
Mother No I can't. I'll have to go and lay down. (*Calling*) Don't be long,
Brenda. (*To Dilys*) Make sure she's straight behind me.

Mother exits

Brenda enters with a cup of water

Brenda Dil, you know tomorrow when you finish work . . . (*She looks at
Dilys*) What's the matter?
Dilys (*pulling herself together*) Nothing, why?
Brenda You've been crying.
Dilys No I haven't.
Brenda Your eyes are all wet.
Dilys (*changing the subject*) I've got a bone to pick with you.

They look at each other

Sophie.
Brenda Well I don't like her.
Dilys What's wrong with her?
Brenda She called me strange. I was in the kitchen but I heard her.

Dilys I'd call you more than strange if you were as obnoxious to me as you
were with her.
Brenda (*after a slight pause*) I'm sorry.

They both smile

Dilys Wash or wipe.
Brenda Wash.

They begin to clear away the dishes

Dil, is she your best friend?
Dilys Sort of.
Brenda I've got a best friend.
Dilys Sandra Evans?
Brenda No. Trevor's mine.
Dilys But he's your brother.
Brenda Never mind. It doesn't make any difference, he can still be my best
friend. If Sophie's your "sort of" best friend, who's your real one?
Dilys Never you mind.
Brenda Is it that Yank?
Dilys How do you know about him?
Brenda It's no secret. Everybody knows he's taking you out. Is it him, Dil,
or isn't it?
Dilys Let's get on with the dishes.
Brenda What's he like, Dil?
Dilys (*thinking about it then smiling to herself*) He's lovely.
Brenda Sandra Evans said he was nice.
Dilys How would she know?
Brenda She saw you together the other night. I like the way they talk I do.
Their accents.
Dilys You've heard one you've heard them all. There's more to a Yank than
the sound of his voice.
Brenda What do you like about yours then?
Dilys Mind your business.

Dilys goes into the kitchen

Brenda Are you going to marry him, Dil?
Dilys (*off*) Don't be silly.
Brenda Why not? They wouldn't have to ask me twice.
Dilys (*off*) You shouldn't be saying things like that.
Brenda Just think—if you did marry him—after the war he'd take you back
to live in America.
Dilys (*off*) I can think of nicer places to live.
Brenda Than America?
Dilys (*off*) It's not like you see it in the films, you know.

Dilys comes out of the kitchen

Brenda I bet it's better than this place. Marry him, Dil and take me with
you.

Dilys (*shouting*) I'm not going to marry him.
Brenda (*amazed at her explosion*) All right—don't shout. It's not my fault if
he hasn't asked you.

Mother knocks on the floor of the bedroom

There you are, you've started Mammy off now.
Dilys (*handing Brenda plates, cups and saucers*) Take these to the kitchen.

Brenda exits to the kitchen with crockery

Dilys pulls herself together a little

Brenda returns

Brenda Will you come and light the gas? I can't do it.
Dilys I'm sorry I shouted.
Brenda It's all right.

They look at each other

Dilys He's already married.
Brenda Does Mammy know?
Dilys Mrs Condon told her tonight.

Brenda stares at Dilys for a moment before speaking

Brenda Dil, you know that brooch I've got?
Dilys Which one?
Brenda That cameo with a nice clasp.
Dilys That's my favourite.
Brenda I want you to have it.
Dilys Why?
Brenda Will you take it?
Dilys What do you want to give it to me for?
Brenda I just want you to have it that's all.
Dilys You'll be sorry.
Brenda No I won't, not ever.
Dilys What's come over you all of a sudden?
Brenda And you know that bracelet, the one I had for Christmas the year
before last?
Dilys Yes.
Brenda I'm giving that to Mammy.
Dilys But she gave it to you.
Brenda I want her to have it back.
Dilys What's the matter with you?
Brenda I don't know what I'm going to give Sandra Evans yet but I'm
giving Trevor my cross and chain.
Dilys What's going on, Brenda?
Brenda (*after a slight pause*) Are you afraid to die, Dil?
Dilys That's a funny question.
Brenda Are you?
Dilys I don't know.

Brenda Do you think Daddy was?

Dilys I don't think about it.

Brenda I do. I often think about whether he was or not. Do you think he was?

Dilys Perhaps. I don't know. No.

Brenda It's only the first thought of it that's frightening. I didn't think Daddy was going to die. I was sure he wasn't. (*After a slight pause*) Not like me. I know I am.

Dilys What do you mean?

Brenda I'm going to die, Dil.

Dilys Don't be silly.

Brenda No, I am honest. I think I must have swallowed some broken glass.

Dilys Broken glass?

Brenda I don't know how. I don't remember doing it.

Dilys You can't have.

Brenda I have. Truly, Dil. Ten fingers up to God. That's why I didn't go to the pictures. I . . . I got ready too. I went and had my bath . . . and then it started.

Dilys (*after pausing*) Oh Brend. It's all right. There's nothing wrong. It happens to every girl.

Brenda (*looking at Dilys distastefully*) Why?

Dilys (*a little lost for words*) Well . . . it just does, that's all.

Brenda It's a funny thing to happen.

Dilys Not really.

Brenda Did it happen to you?

Dilys Yes.

Brenda And to Mammy?

Dilys nods

I think it's awful.

Dilys It's not very pleasant I know.

Brenda Thank God it's stopped anyway.

Dilys Oh it'll start again.

Brenda (*shocked*) When?

Dilys Soon.

Brenda Honest?

Dilys You'll be like that for a couple of days.

Brenda It will stop though, won't it?

Dilys Yes.

Brenda is relieved

Until next month.

Brenda What happens then?

Dilys It starts all over again.

Brenda Oh no!

Dilys Listen, Brend. All women have them.

Brenda What?

Dilys It's called a period.

Brenda What do men have?
Dilys Nothing.
Brenda That's not fair.
Dilys Maybe not but that's how it is. Come on let's go to bed. I'd better put you right.
Brenda Put me right?
Dilys Give you something to wear.
Brenda But I've already got my bed clothes on.
Dilys I mean a belt.

Brenda makes a face, not really understanding

Brenda What about the dishes?
Dilys Leave them.
Brenda You can tell Mammy in the morning then, right?
Dilys Come on.
Brenda Hey, Dil, now I know I'm not going to die—it means I can keep my brooch, doesn't it?
Dilys (*laughing*) Let's go up.
Brenda What is it called again?
Dilys A period.
Brenda Why is it called that?
Dilys (*going to the kitchen and switching off the light*) Because it happens periodically.
Brenda (*not understanding*) What?
Dilys Every month.
Brenda What about my bath?
Dilys (*opening the passage door*) What about it?
Brenda Did that have anything to do with it?
Dilys It might have.

She switches the living-room light off. The room can only be seen now through a dim orange glow from the dying fire. Dilys's and Brenda's voices disappear as they ascend the stairs

(*Off*) You shouldn't wash when you're like that anyway.
Brenda (*off*) Why?
Dilys (*off*) Well because you shouldn't. It's messy.
Brenda (*off*) What about my face?
Dilys (*off; laughing*) Yes, you can wash that.
Brenda (*off*) And my feet?

CURTAIN

SCENE 2

The same. Early August, afternoon

Greg is sitting in the armchair. After he has been there for some time, he rises and walks aimlessly around the room. He eventually finds himself at the sideboard. He picks up a photograph and looks at it as ...

Dilys enters from upstairs. The atmosphere is somewhat uneasy. Dilys pulls the curtain across the door

Dilys She should sleep for a bit now.
Greg Did you give her the candy?
Dilys She said thank you.
Greg I bet she doesn't eat it.
Dilys She doesn't like it. She'll give it to Brenda.
Greg I haven't scored there, have I?
Dilys She's afraid, that's all. Afraid I'll get hurt.
Greg You're not afraid, are you?
Dilys Not yet.
Greg That implies you will be.

She doesn't answer

Are you working Sunday?

Dilys shakes her head

Take you dancing?
Dilys Lovely.

There is a pause in which Greg comes to sit on the settee

Greg I had a letter from Evelyn yesterday.

Dilys doesn't answer

She wants to sell the house and move back to New Jersey.
Dilys Where her mother lives?
Greg Right.
Dilys (*after a slight pause*) Do you think she suspects anything?
Greg Oh I think she might.
Dilys (*after a slight pause*) Are you going to let her?

He looks at her

Move back to New Jersey?
Greg She lives in a beautiful house.
Dilys Evelyn?
Greg Her mother.

An awkward pause

Dilys I wish Brenda would hurry with the meat.
Greg There's no rush. I don't have to be back until four.
Dilys I've got to cook it for Trevor's tea.

They stare at each other for a moment

Greg Why don't you come and sit down.

She joins him on the settee. He takes her hand

Dilys Brenda might come in any minute.

Greg We're not doing anything wrong.

They stare into each other's eyes

Yeah.

Dilys Yes what?

Greg Yeah I'm gonna let her move back to New Jersey.

Dilys Should that mean something?

Greg Do you want it to?

She doesn't answer

I want it too. (*A slight pause*) It means that Evelyn suspects a little of what's going on. It means that she's not in a position to do anything about it and wants to move near her momma in case things don't work out.

Dilys looks away but looks back as he begins to speak

It also means if I let her go a kind of admission. (*A slight pause*) On the other hand — if I say "stay", that means it's OK. Everything's under control.

They stare at each other again before he kisses her. The front door slams and they spring apart

Brenda enters with a parcel of meat

Brenda I queued for over an hour at the butcher's. (*She puts the meat down on the table*)

Dilys I wish you wouldn't slam the front door. You know Mammy's in bed.

Brenda It's only flu.

Dilys Never mind.

Brenda Hello Greg.

Greg Hi!

Brenda You should have seen the size of it.

Dilys What?

Brenda The queue. It stretched right down Bute Street, down Crown Avenue and half way up Phillips Terrace.

Dilys What meat did you get?

Brenda I had a lovely piece, very lean and it was cheap. I'll put the book and the change here. (*She does*) The butcher said it would fry lovely. (*A slight pause*) Hey, I walked back up the street with Sandra. You know her, Dil. Her sister married one of them Yanks from the camp.

Dilys Sylvia?

Brenda That's right. Anyway, she was telling me that they're all going away soon.

Dilys looks at her

The Yanks I mean.

Dilys (*to Greg*) Is that right?

Greg It's the first I've heard of it.

Dilys (*to Brenda*) When?

Brenda She didn't say. She just said that she heard her sister telling her mother that it won't be long before they'll be on the move. (*In an American accent*) I guess her husband must have told her.

Greg It's coming along. Sounds a little Southern here and there but you're picking it up just fine.

Dilys (*to Greg*) You're sure you haven't heard anything?

Greg We hear things all the time, but it's all rumour. Sure we're gonna move. We knew that before we came, but we don't know when and we won't know either until twenty-four hours before. Maybe it's gonna be Saturday—maybe it's gonna be six months Saturday.

Brenda (*after a slight pause*) Well that's what Sandra said anyway.

Dilys (*a little shaken*) Go and make the beds, Brend.

Brenda They're done. We did them together this morning.

Dilys Wash the dishes then.

Brenda There's none dirty.

Dilys (*shouting*) Well go down the shops.

Brenda (*shouting back*) What are you shouting for?

Dilys looks at Greg then tries to pull herself together

I'm not going down the shop again. I've only just come back.

Dilys (*still looking at Greg*) Fetch potatoes.

Brenda Fetch them yourself.

Dilys And we need more bread.

Brenda *I'm* not going.

Dilys Trevor doesn't like it stale.

Brenda Can I have threepence?

Dilys Don't be silly.

Brenda Well I'm not going then.

Dilys Please, Brend?

Brenda No, I'm not.

Greg takes a bar of chocolate out of his pocket

I'm sure you think that's all I'm here for. I'm forever going up and down the shop. Well you've had it. I'm in now and I'm not going back out . . . (*She sees the chocolate that Greg is holding out in front of him*) What was it you said you wanted?

Dilys A loaf of bread and potatoes.

Greg tosses the chocolate to Brenda and she catches it

Take the money from the sideboard.

Brenda (*doing so*) Do you want anything else while I'm down there? You'd better say now if there is because I'm not going down again today.

Dilys No that's everything.

Brenda goes

There is a pause

Greg Are you OK?
Dilys (*after a slight pause*) Yes.
Greg Dil?

She doesn't look at him

I'm gonna have to go away at sometime.
Dilys I know.
Greg I'm coming back.
Dilys Of course you are. (*Upset*) This bloody war.
Greg If it wasn't for the war I wouldn't be here. It won't be for long. Try
and look on me as a kinda . . . kinda library book. I'm going out on loan,
that's all. It'll be all right. It'll work out. I promise.
Dilys No-one has the right to promise anything these days. It's not only the
war. There's Evelyn.
Greg Forget about Evelyn.
Dilys How can you say that? How can we forget about her?

She is about to move away but he holds her close to him

Greg It's easy. I love you.

They stare at each other for a moment

The door opens and Mother enters

Dilys What are you doing out of bed?
Mother It's no good I can't rest.
Dilys Come on, I'll take you back up.
Mother No I'm down now. I may as well stay down.
Dilys You'll be warmer in bed.
Mother You've got a tidy fire down here.

There is a pause

Dilys Tea anyone?
Greg Not for me thanks.
Dilys Mam?
Mother All right.

Dilys looks at the two of them then goes to the kitchen

Greg (*after a slight pause*) Would you like a blanket round your shoulders,
ma'am?
Mother I'm not cold.
Greg (*taking her arm and kneeling beside her*) I thought maybe these were
goose pimples.

*She looks at him very gently then tries to retrieve her arms but he holds on. She
looks at him again*

She's very special to me. I promise I won't do anything to hurt her.

Mother No-one should——

Greg —promise anything these days. I know.

Mother What about your wife? (*Taking her arm away*) Did you promise not to hurt her too?

Greg I made a mistake, ma'am. We all do that sometimes.

Mother When the war is over and you go back home you'll feel different.

Greg What if I don't.

Mother Then you must make yourself.

Greg I won't give her up.

Mother It will only hurt for a little while.

Greg Begging your pardon, ma'am, but how can you say that?

Mother I'm telling you within twelve months of you going away it will fizzle out.

Greg It wouldn't be fair for me to try and speak for Dilys but—as far as I'm concerned I can assure you . . . (*He finds it difficult to find the words*) . . . Both families wanted the marriage. I was pressurized from all angles.

Mother You mean you didn't want to marry her?

Greg Yes. I don't know. I suppose I did. I thought I loved her at the time.

Mother And now you've met Dilys——

Greg And now I know how I should have felt.

There is a pause

I *know* my responsibilities but that doesn't stop me loving Dilys. I didn't kid her along. As soon as I realized we were getting serious I told her my situation. We knew the score. We went into this thing with both eyes wide open.

Mother That still doesn't make it right.

Greg What's right or wrong really hasn't anything to do with it. It's not right that men can kill each other but it's going on every day. Maybe what Dilys and I feel for each other is wrong. But at least we didn't make it happen. It just did. Not like this stupid war.

Mother If Dilys is half as special to you as you say she is then you'll finish it now. It will be easier for her to hear you say it than for you to go off one day, and she'd be hanging around waiting for your letters. Suspecting a change in your attitude. Looking at the first letter and comparing it to the latest and realizing how less and less "passionate" if that's the right word, they've become. Hurt her now, while I'm well enough to help her through it.

Greg (*after a slight pause*) I'm sorry, ma'am.

Dilys enters

Dilys Are you sure you won't have a——

Greg I have to go now.

He leaves

Dilys (*calling*) Greg! (*Opening the door*) Greg! I'll see you on Sunday.

Mother Leave him go.

Dilys If you mess this up for me . . .

The front door slams

Mother Where are you going on Sunday?
Dilys Dancing.
Mother If he thinks anything of you you'll see him before then.
Dilys I wouldn't be surprised if I never saw him again.
Mother So you really think I've frightened him off?
Dilys I don't know what you've said to him.
Mother I only told him to leave you alone. To break it off now before it hurts.
Dilys (*sarcastic*) Oh is that all.
Mother If he takes my advice, Dilys, you're better off without him. If he is going to be frightened off by me then he's not worth having anyway.
Dilys Is that what it was, a test?
Mother No. Oh I don't know. (*Sighing*) I wish I knew what you want out of it.
Dilys (*after a slight pause*) There's talk they're moving soon.
Mother The Yanks?

Dilys nods

Did he tell you that?
Dilys No Brenda. Sandra Evans told her. Her sister married one.
Mother What did he say to that?
Dilys Greg said it was a rumour. It's only a matter of time though. We know that.
Mother What are you going to do then?
Dilys (*after a slight pause*) I don't know.
Mother You'll be all right, won't you?

Dilys doesn't answer

Perhaps you'd better ease off. What if he ends up breaking your heart?
Dilys That's all part of it. I think every girl should have her heart broken at least once. (*After a slight pause*) I don't think I meant that.
Mother Do you love him, Dil?
Dilys Yes.
Mother How do you know?
Dilys How does anyone know? How did you know you loved Daddy?

Mother looks away

Do you remember when you first met him? When he first looked at you — I mean really looked at you, and you knew he saw right down into your soul? Do you remember how your chest felt funny, and your heart raced, your breath left you for a second and your stomach began to shake from the inside? I've been seeing Greg for months and I feel like that every time I look at him.
Mother If I'd felt like that every time I looked at your father I'd have seen a doctor.

Dilys I didn't love him straightaway. He was just another fella—another Yank. But the more I got to know him and the more he made me laugh ... he's not just another Yank at all.

Mother (*after a slight pause*) I think the kettle's boiling.

Dilys Why don't you go back to bed and I'll bring your tea up to you?

Mother I'm fed up with that room. I'm glad to come down for a change of scenery. What time is it?

Dilys Twenty-five past two.

Mother You'd better start Trevor's food.

Dilys There's plenty of time.

Mother What have you got for him?

Dilys Chips. Brenda fetched some meat from the butcher's.

Mother What meat?

Dilys I don't know. Brenda said the butcher said it would fry lovely.

Mother Where is it?

Dilys (*going to the kitchen*) On the table.

Mother Let's have a look at it.

Dilys You'll have to wait a minute.

She exits to the kitchen

Mother Sausages I thought he was having.

Dilys (*off*) That's what I told her to bring, but she said they were all queuing for that.

Mother It would hardly be steak, would it?

Dilys enters carrying two cups and saucers and the packet of meat

Dilys Have a look. (*She puts down the crockery and hands the packet of meat to her mother*)

Mother I hope it's not gristly whatever it is, you know Trevor and fat.

Dilys Brenda's pretty good. I don't think she'd fetch rubbish.

Mother (*waving her hand in the air*) You've got to watch these flies. I'm sure we've had that big blue one in here for a fortnight. (*She opens the packet and looks at the meat*) Hey, you can't give this to Trevor.

Dilys Why not?

Mother Well look at it.

Dilys (*doing so*) There's nothing wrong with it. It's a lovely piece of meat.

Mother You know what it is, do you?

Dilys It looks like steak to me.

Mother It's too dark for steak.

Dilys What is it then?

Mother Horse.

Dilys pauses and looks at it

Dilys Is it?

Mother You've only got to look at the colour and the size of it.

Dilys Can you eat horse?

Mother They say it's a bit on the sweet side.

Dilys But you can eat it though?

Mother Oh yes.

Dilys Perhaps Trevor will enjoy it.

Mother Trevor won't eat it. He'll go off his head if you give him that.

Dilys We won't tell him. You can't waste a nice bit of meat like that, it's too good.

Mother You know how fussy he is with food.

Dilys There's a war on, you can't afford to be fussy.

Mother Well I don't want anything to do with it. If you give it to him and he finds out—you don't want to tell him to come and see me. I'll swear I know nothing about it.

Dilys He won't find out. How will he find out?

Mother Does Brenda know what she's fetched?

Dilys If she asks anything I'll tell her the same as I'll tell Trevor, it's best steak. I'll fry it with half an onion and nobody'll know the difference.

Mother I wonder where he had it from.

Dilys Who?

Mother The butcher.

Dilys The same place as he gets all his meat, I expect.

Mother I doubt if *that* came from the slaughter house.

Dilys Why?

Mother Well . . . I mean . . . they don't slaughter horses . . . do they?

Dilys What do they do then?

Mother (*mysteriously*) I don't know.

Dilys How else would they kill them?

Mother Perhaps it wasn't "killed".

Dilys (*after a slight pause*) You mean perhaps——

Mother It just . . . died. Of its own accord.

Dilys (*making a face*) Oh, do you think so? (*Looking at the meat*) What part of the horse would you say it was from?

Mother Looking at the shape of it I'd say it was rump.

Dilys Rump horse. It doesn't sound very nice. (*She takes the meat from her mother*)

Mother Never mind what it sounds like, you make sure you fry enough onion so's that Trevor doesn't find out.

Dilys I wouldn't mind trying a bit myself, but it's the thought of it that puts me off.

Mother I don't see why, you've eaten bacon and rabbit.

Dilys But they seem different somehow.

Mother Cover it up now, Dilys, before the flies have it. I'm sick of them. Send Brenda down the road this afternoon for fly paper. If I don't kill that big blue one soon I don't know what I'll do. I'm sure he fancies me. I went up to bed last night and he followed me.

Dilys How many shall we get?

Mother Better get four. We can have two in here, one in the kitchen and one in my bedroom then.

The front door slams and Brenda enters like a hurricane. She is breathless but still hurries around the room holding on to the furniture as she tries unsuccessfully to get her words out

Dilys Take your time, take your time.

Mother What's the matter with you?

Brenda tries to tell them but is still fighting for breath

Sit down and get your breath back.

Brenda reacts to this but is adamant to get her words out

Dilys Shall I fetch you a glass of water?

Brenda shakes her head

Mother Take the goods off her, Dilys.

Dilys does. Brenda manages to squeeze out the word "purse"

What did she say?

Dilys I think she said purse.

Mother (*to Brenda*) Purse?

Brenda (*very breathlessly*) Money.

Dilys Money?

Mother What does she want money for?

Brenda Quick!

Dilys What's the matter?

Brenda Give me money.

Mother What for?

Brenda (*finally shouting her words*) There's bananas in the Co-op! (*Pronounced "Cop"*)

Mother Oh we can't afford them.

Brenda But I've never had one.

Mother Then you won't know what you've missed.

Brenda It's not fair, Sandra Evans' mother bought six.

Mother I can't help that.

Brenda I never get anything.

Mother Perhaps I'll get you one for your stocking come Christmas.

Brenda Everybody's buying them now. There's a huge queue.

Dilys Then they'll probably be all gone by the time you get back down there.

Brenda (*to Mother*) I bet Dilys has tasted one.

Dilys No, I haven't.

Brenda You wouldn't say if you had, not to make a row.

Dilys It's you who's making the row.

Brenda Well if you can afford meat for Trevor why can't you afford a rotten stinking banana for me?

Mother Trevor's working and earning money, Brenda. You're still a little girl in school.

Brenda If Daddy was here he'd buy me one.

Mother Well he's not and that's an end to it. You'd better start doing something with that meat, Dilys.

Dilys Have we got any onions?

Brenda Well if we haven't *I'm* not fetching any.

Mother And less of that cheek.

Brenda I've been down the road four times today already.
Mother And you'll go another four times if I want you to. Have a look in
the pantry, Dilys. There should be one under the stone.

Dilys exits to the kitchen

It's a good job your father's not here to hear the way you talk to me.
Brenda He would have bought me one.
Dilys (*calling from the pantry*) Is this all right on the window sill?
Mother Yes. Llew the fruit only brought it last week.
Brenda Have you heard about him? Well not him, his horse. Dolly.

There is a pause. Mother looks at her

She's dead.

Dilys appears from the kitchen

Mother Are you sure?
Brenda Sandra's mother was telling me when I met her in the queue. She
said he went to take her out last night and found her dead in the stable.
Mother (*after a slight pause*) What are you going to do now, Dilys?
Brenda I liked old Dolly too. She was a nice old thing.
Dilys Perhaps we'd better give him beans instead.
Mother (*in a temper*) That's her fault that is. (*To Brenda*) How much did
you give for that meat?
Brenda What meat?
Mother (*shouting*) Trevor's meat.
Brenda Half a crown.
Mother (*still in a temper*) Half a crown and we'll have to give it to the dog.
Brenda Why?
Dilys He can eat it fried. (*She picks up the parcel*) Dolly or not.
Brenda Dolly?
Mother (*shouting to Dilys*) You've bloody done it now, haven't you?
Dilys You'd better tell her to keep her mouth shut.

Dilys exits to the kitchen with the meat

Brenda What does she mean "Dolly"?
Mother One word from you to Trevor about that meat and you'll have the
finest hammering you've ever had.
Brenda I wish I knew what was going on.
Mother It's that meat you fetched.
Brenda What's the matter with it?
Mother There's nothing the matter with it. It's just Dolly's arse end that's
all.
Brenda What Dolly?
Mother (*shouting*) The horse. Dolly the horse. The one who brings the veg.
Or used to. That butcher sold you horse meat.
Brenda Well it's not my fault.
Mother You should watch what you're buying.

Brenda She only died last night. Oh well at least you know it's fresh. How do you know it's Dolly anyway?

Dilys enters

Dilys We don't. We're just putting two and two together.
Brenda Well you can't give it to Trevor.
Dilys Why not?
Brenda Because he doesn't like horse.
Dilys He liked Dolly.
Brenda I liked Dolly, but that doesn't mean I want to eat her.
Dilys You heard what Mammy said. Trevor's not to know.
Brenda Well I'm going to tell him.
Mother You do!
Brenda I am.
Mother I warned you what would happen.
Brenda I reckon it's worth a hiding.
Mother (*to Dilys*) This is all your fault.
Dilys She bought the stuff not me.
Mother You had to open your mouth.
Dilys I couldn't help it, it was an accident.
Mother Well you'll have to give it to the dog now. Trevor would go up the wall if you gave it to him and he found out what it was.
Brenda You don't have to give it to the dog. You could still give it to Trevor. If you filled my mouth.
Mother Filled your mouth?
Brenda (*smiling*) With a banana.

Mother looks at Dilys and sighs heavily at being blackmailed

Mother I don't know who she's following. Where's my purse?
Brenda (*handing it to her immediately*) Here it is.
Mother (*giving Brenda money*) Here. And one word about it to Trevor and you'll eat that banana, skin and all.

Brenda smiles at them both sweetly, as she exits singing, rather loudly, "Goodbye Dolly I Must Leave You"

Mother looks at Dilys and they both laugh as the Lights dim to a Black-out

CURTAIN

ACT II

SCENE 1

The same. An hour or so later

Dilys is peeling potatoes at the table. Brenda is sitting in the armchair looking at her banana

Dilys So you won't go then?

Brenda Definitely not.

Dilys Not even for a penny?

Brenda I'm not going back down the shops. Not even if you give me a shilling.

Dilys Oh well it's you who's going to have to face Mammy, not me.

Brenda Look, I've offered to kill them with a piece of cardboard.

Dilys Fly paper Mammy asked for and fly paper she wants.

Brenda They're a waste of money.

Dilys If anything's a waste of money it's that banana.

Brenda I wonder what they're like.

Dilys It's a funny kind of taste really.

Brenda Ha ha! Caught you. So you have tasted one. I knew you were telling me lies.

Dilys I wish you'd either put it away or eat it.

Brenda Oh I'm going to eat it. Well not yet anyway. I might eat it later on, or I might even keep it till tomorrow.

There is a knock at the front door

Dilys Answer it, Brend.

Brenda leaves to answer the door. She doesn't return

After a moment Greg enters

Greg Hi!

Dilys stops chipping potatoes and looks at him

I called back. I felt I should.

Dilys Are you staying?

Greg Yeah. But I haven't got long.

Dilys Sit down then. Where's Brenda?

Greg She's gone for a walk. I asked her to. (*After a slight pause*) She told me your mamma had gone back to bed.

Dilys Is there anything wrong?

Greg I don't know. I don't think so. (*He stares at her for a moment*) Yes. I lost the first round.

Dilys She told me what she said to you.

Greg More than anything I don't want you to get hurt.

Dilys She said it was all a test. She said if you really thought anything of me I'd see you before Sunday.

Greg A test?

Dilys (*taking off her mother*) "If he's going to be frightened off by me, Dilys, then he's not worth having anyway." (*She tries to laugh*)

Greg What if I hadn't called back? I nearly didn't, you know.

Dilys It wouldn't have made any difference. I never listen to her.

Greg I just don't want you to get hurt. I've never said anything to you I didn't mean, and I've never made any promises I didn't try to keep. (*After a slight pause*) It's a terrible chance we're taking.

Dilys We're not taking any chances we don't want to take, are we?

Greg (*after a slight pause*) No.

Dilys If you're looking for a get-out——

Greg I'm not.

Dilys It's the easiest thing in the world to finish it. It's the dealing with finishing it that's difficult.

Greg I don't want to finish it, Dil.

Dilys Are you sure?

Greg (*taking a letter from his inside pocket*) I'm letting her move back to New Jersey, aren't I?

Dilys Have you written to her already?

Greg I wrote it this morning, before I talked with your mamma.

Dilys Before you even spoke to me then?

Greg It was the easiest letter I've ever written. It's mailing it that's going to be the problem. I want what's best for you. That's why I've decided *not* to mail it.

She looks at him

I'm gonna leave that to you. (*He puts the letter down on the arm of the settee*)

Dilys That's not fair.

Greg All's fair in——

Dilys You shouldn't expect me to post it.

Greg Dil, I don't expect anything. I just think it would be better if you did it. Then I'm not pushing.

Dilys (*after a slight pause*) What if I don't post it?

Greg Then Evelyn won't move back to New Jersey. (*He pauses*) She'll stay and expect me home.

Dilys Shouldn't we be making this decision together?

Greg You know what I want.

Dilys (*pausing before speaking*) Do I?

Greg (*after a slight pause*) Brenda's friend, the one whose sister married one of us, the Yank? There might be something in what he said. There's a lot

of activity going on at the camp. Something's happening. It might well be
that we're moving off.
Dilys (*after a slight pause*) If you are will I see you before you go?
Greg I hope so.
Dilys Will I?
Greg (*after a slight pause*) I don't know. But you can be sure of one thing, if
there's any chance I'll be here.
Dilys (*crying*) What about Sunday?
Greg Dancing?

She nods

Let's keep our fingers crossed.
Dilys (*after a pause*) Greg?

He looks at her

Come and put your arms around me.

He does so, standing behind her

Hold me tightly.
Greg I am.
Dilys Tighter.

He does. They begin to sway as if they are about to dance

This is it, Greg. I know it is.

They begin to dance as Greg opens his eyes

Greg Everything's gonna be all right. You're gonna be just fine you'll see.
Dilys It's not me I'm worried about. What about us?
Greg (*turning her to face him*) You just be sure to mail it.
Dilys (*still upset*) I didn't think I'd ... It's not supposed to be like this. I
shouldn't feel ... (*Angry with her own emotion*) I wanted it to be ... (*She
breaks down*) Oh God.
Greg Dil? Dil, I'm gonna have to go. Now.

They look at each other

The front door slams and Sophie enters

This time they don't spring apart

Sophie Dil ... have you seen them ... have you heard? Oh hiya, Greg, you
already know then?
Dilys What about?
Sophie I rushed up to tell you about the Yanks but I suppose Greg has
already told you. Trevor's not home yet?
Dilys No. He won't be long though.
Sophie Has he said anything?
Dilys Who?
Sophie Trevor.
Dilys About what?
Sophie Me. Well and him. Us, you know. Has he mentioned anything?

Dilys No.

Sophie You'll never guess what happened last night.

Greg (*intimately to Dilys*) I have to go.

Sophie It just came out of the blue. I didn't expect it at all.

Dilys (*to Greg*) No. Not yet. Please.

Sophie We were just walking home and we were half-way up Rotherham Street. We were standing outside number seventeen.

Greg kisses Dilys

That's going to be my lucky number from now on; and Dil, you'll never guess what he said to me. He said, "How old are you?" I said that's not a very nice question to ask a lady. He said, "How old are you?" And I said twenty-eight. Then he never said anything for a minute; but then he said "Twenty-eight?" And I just looked at him.

Greg breaks away from Dilys and leaves

And he said "I think we'd better get married." Well Dil, I couldn't believe my ears. You could have knocked me down with a sledge-hammer. Then he said to think it over. But I told him I didn't want to think it over, I told him I'd marry him there and then. (*She looks at Dilys, and sees that she is crying*) Oh don't cry for me, Dil. This is the happiest day of my life. Where's Greg?

Dilys He had to go.

Sophie Well, aren't you going to wish me luck?

Dilys Wish you luck? What for?

Sophie For my wedding, stupid. Haven't you been listening to anything I've been saying?

Dilys You're getting married?

Sophie Yes.

Dilys To who?

Sophie Trevor, who else? I still can't believe it. I would have thought I'd dreamt it but I haven't slept all night.

Dilys I'm really happy for you, Soph.

Sophie You should have seen my mother. She almost fainted when I told her.

Dilys What did your father say?

Sophie I haven't told him yet. I'll leave it till he's sober.

Dilys Trevor hasn't said a word here. That's just like him though he's a real dark horse.

Sophie Have you heard about Llew the fruit.

Dilys Yes, he's dead isn't he?

Sophie Well not him, his horse.

Dilys He found her in the stable.

Sophie That's right. Who told you?

Dilys Brenda came in and said.

Sophie Where's your mother—in bed?

Dilys (*nodding*) She hasn't long gone up.

Sophie Trevor hasn't told her either then?

Dilys I don't think so.

Sophie Shall I go up and say something?

Dilys No leave it for now. Let her get some sleep.

Sophie (*after a slight pause*) What are you doing—Trevor's dinner?

Dilys nods

What's he having?

Dilys Steak and onions and chips.

Sophie Steak? Where did you have that from?

Dilys Brenda fetched it.

Sophie Well he can make the most of it. We won't be able to afford for him to eat like that when he's married to me.

Dilys You are sure about it, Soph, aren't you?

Sophie About what?

Dilys About what he said. Trevor. You haven't got it wrong?

Sophie (*laughing*) Don't be daft, no of course I haven't. (*She laughs again then stops abruptly*) You don't think I have, do you?

Dilys I don't know what he said.

Sophie I told you how it was. We were walking up Rotherham Street and he stops and asks me my age. I told him and he said, "I think we'd better get married." I couldn't have got that wrong, could I?

Dilys doesn't answer

Could I?

Dilys It sounds a bit odd.

Sophie (*a little angry*) Well it didn't sound odd last night.

Dilys We'll just have to wait and see that's all.

Sophie Wait and see what?

Dilys What Trevor says.

Sophie I bet I have got it wrong. That's just like me. That's the whole way my life's been going. If he did say it, he could deny it and I don't want to force him into anything. That's not true, I would. (*After a slight pause*) When is he going, Dil?

Dilys looks at her

Greg?

Dilys He's gone.

Sophie Gone? Won't you be seeing him, before he goes off?

Dilys I shouldn't think so.

Sophie Oh Dil. Did I barge in on you two? I'd never have done it if I'd known. Well I mean I knew they were moving that's one of the reasons I called. I had no idea he was saying goodbye. Why didn't you chuck me out?

Dilys If I had you'd never have understood.

Sophie I wouldn't have invited you to the wedding but I'd have got over it. (*She laughs*) I'm sorry, Dil. Honest. It's going to be all right though, isn't it? I mean he is going to write?

Dilys That depends on me and the postman. (*She picks up the letter that Greg left and puts it in the sideboard drawer*)

Sophie I don't get that. How can Greg writing to you depend on you and the postman.

Dilys It's a long story.

Sophie If you like later on, I'll come up with you to the camp. We can watch them driving past. You never know, you might catch a glimpse of him as he goes.

Dilys Only a glimpse of him I've had.

Sophie Do you want to do that?

Dilys I don't know. I'll think about it.

Sophie It's going to be quiet around this place once they've gone.

Dilys Back to the old days.

Sophie (*after a slight pause*) Is there anything I can do? Shall I help with Trevor's dinner?

Dilys It's all done now. I've only got to put them in the pan.

She goes to the kitchen

Sophie That steak smells lovely.

The front door slams

Dilys (*off*) Do you want a taste?

Sophie No, I'd better not.

Dilys (*off*) Trevor won't mind you having a bit.

Sophie I bet he won't.

Dilys (*off*) What?

Sophie No—it's all right—leave it.

Brenda enters, peeping her head around the door first

Brenda Psst!

Sophie looks for the noise

Psst!

Sophie picks up the tablecloth and looks under there

Psst!

Sophie looks towards the door and sees Brenda

Sophie Oh it's you.

Dilys (*off*) What?

Brenda Has he gone?

Sophie Who?

Dilys (*off*) Did you say something?

Sophie It's all right, it's Brenda.

Brenda Greg.

Sophie Yes, he went a couple of minutes ago.

Brenda comes into the room

What have you got there?

Brenda Wait a minute and I'll show you. I can't get the lid open. Can you do it? (*She hands a tea-tin to Sophie*)

Sophie It's very heavy. What have you got in there, lead?

She opens the tin and hands it back to Brenda. Brenda takes it and opens the contents on the table. The tin was full of pennies

Brenda Look at all this.

Sophie Where did you get it from? (*Calling*) Dilys, come and have a look at this.

Brenda There must be at least two pounds here.

Dilys enters from the kitchen

Dilys What is it?

She looks at Sophie and Sophie nods towards the table. Dilys sees the money

Where did you get all that?

Brenda Greg gave it to me. When I answered the door to him he asked me if I'd go for a walk. When I said I would he gave me this tin. The thing was—I couldn't walk too far it was heavy.

Sophie There must be at least three pounds there.

Brenda As much as that?

Dilys (*to Brenda*) Put it back in the tin. You can't count it there—I'm setting the table.

Brenda Oh . . . but I've got it all out now.

Dilys I can't help that.

Brenda There's no need to be funny. He gave me something for you too.

Dilys looks at Brenda, then Sophie, then back to Brenda

I didn't have a pocket so I kept it in my hand. (*She opens her fist and shows Dilys*)

Sophie What is it?

Dilys It's a stamp.

Brenda My palm is sticky.

Dilys peels off the stamp

Sophie What did he give you that for?

Brenda I'm going to wash my hands.

Brenda exits to the kitchen

Dilys What do you normally have stamps for.

Sophie That's a funny present if you ask me.

Dilys No it's not. (*Taking the letter from the sideboard drawer*) Not really. (*She fixes the stamp to it and puts it back in the drawer*)

Brenda (*off*) This meat smells lovely, Dil.

Sophie Do you want me to post it for you?

Dilys No I don't think so.

Sophie I'm going down there after.

Dilys I'll do it—it's all right. (*She puts the pennies back in the tin*)

Sophie Shall I get Trevor's bath?

Dilys Yes if you like. You know where it is.

Sophie goes off to the kitchen

Give the chips a shake, Brend.

After a few seconds the front door slams and Trevor enters. He is black with coal

You're early.

Trevor I don't think so. What's that smell?

Dilys Your dinner. It won't be long.

Trevor What have I got?

Dilys Steak and chips.

Trevor Steak?

Dilys There's onions too.

Trevor Smells great. Where's Mother?

Dilys In bed.

Trevor Is she any better?

Dilys She's just the same.

Trevor What's the weather been like?

Dilys We had a drop of rain this morning, but it's cleared up nice now. Sophie's here.

Trevor Is she?

Dilys She's outside getting your bath.

Trevor How long has she been here?

Brenda enters

Brenda Hey Dil, does Sophie know about Trevor's meat . . . Oh hiya, Trev.

Trevor How's my favourite sister?

Brenda Rich. Did Dilys tell you?

Trevor No.

Brenda Greg gave me all his pennies. He must have saved them up.

Dilys I've put them back in the tin.

Brenda I want to count them.

Dilys Do it on the chair then.

During the next scene Brenda counts her pennies and places them in shilling piles on the arm of the chair

Brenda Sophie's here, Trev.

Trevor Yeah. Dilys said. What does Sophie know about my meat that I don't?

Dilys (*after a slight pause*) Nothing.

Trevor What was Brenda on about then?

Dilys Oh that it was steak that's all. She queued for hours and managed to get the last piece. Didn't you, Brend?

Brenda (*looking at Dilys then at Trevor before speaking*) Yeah, that's right.

Sophie enters from the kitchen struggling with the bath

Dilys No, no, not in here, Soph. Put it on the table out the back. Trevor'll wash out there in this weather.

Sophie exits with the bath

She wanted to give me a hand. (*After a slight pause*) She's a nice girl, Trevor. I hope you're not going to hurt her.

Brenda How much do you reckon I got here, Trev?

Trevor If it's over a fiver I'll double it.

Brenda Will you?

Dilys Don't listen to him, Brenda, he's teasing you. You've never got a fiver there.

Brenda You won't know till I count it.

There is a slight pause

Dilys I'd better see to the chips.

Dilys goes to the kitchen

Brenda Do you want to help me count it?

Trevor kneels beside the chair and counts money with Brenda. After a few seconds she looks at him

Go and get a chair or have a wash. You look like Al Jolson.

Trevor (*after a slight pause*) Do you like Sophie, Brend?

Brenda She's all right. Do you?

Trevor She's not bad, is she?

Brenda I didn't like her when she first came here.

Trevor I can't say I was all that keen either.

Brenda She sort of grows on you.

Trevor Mammy likes her.

Brenda Like fungus. (*She laughs*) No, I didn't mean that. (*After a slight pause*) Mammy'd like anyone as long as they weren't American or black. Or both. Pile them on the arm. (*After a slight pause*) You like her a lot, don't you?

Trevor (*teasing her*) Mammy? Yeah, she's great.

Brenda No, I mean Sophie.

Trevor (*imitating Al Jolson*) "Mammy? Can you hear me Mammy? Oh. I'm coming."

Brenda laughs

"Wait for me. Wait for me Mammy. Do you hear? Oh."

Suddenly Mother knocks on the bedroom floor above. Trevor stops but they still laugh

Sophie enters from the kitchen

Sophie Is it a solo or can anyone join in?

Trevor I'm just doing one of my impressions.

Brenda You should see the ones he does of you.

Sophie (*laughing*) I bet they're not as good as the ones I do of him. I've put your bath on the table out the back.

Trevor OK, ta.

Sophie Can I help you count them as well?

Trevor Here you are, come by here. I want to wash my face anyway. (*Handing Sophie the pennies he's already counted*) There's a shilling there.

Trevor goes off to the kitchen

Sophie takes his place alongside the armchair

Brenda (*after a slight pause*) He said he'd double it if it's over a fiver.

Sophie I don't think there's that much here. (*After a slight pause*) Did he say anything else?

Brenda Like what?

Sophie Like anything.

Brenda (*after a slight pause*) He asked me if I liked you.

Sophie Yeah.

Brenda Then I asked him if he liked you.

Sophie What did he say? No wait. I don't want to know. (*After a slight pause*) Yes I do. I've changed my mind. Tell me.

Brenda He didn't answer me he just broke into song.

Sophie Well that's a good sign. Are you sure he didn't say anything else.

Brenda He said you grew on him.

Sophie (*pleased*) Did he?

Brenda Yeah, no wait a minute. I think I said that.

Sophie Did he agree with you?

Brenda I can't remember.

Sophie Well did he disagree with you?

Brenda I don't know.

Sophie Well either he did or he didn't.

Brenda I was counting. My head was full of figures.

Sophie You're a great help you are.

Brenda Don't blame me. Everybody blames me. It's always my fault. I had the blame for Trevor's meat.

Trevor enters

Trevor Who blamed you for my meat?

Brenda Mammy.

Dilys pops her head in from the kitchen

She blamed me for spending all that money on best steak.

Dilys pops back into the kitchen

Didn't she, Dil?

Trevor Whose banana?

Brenda Mine. Will you pass it to me? I think I'd better eat it before——

Trevor Before what?

Brenda Before I finish counting my money.

He hands it to her

Ta. (*During the following, she peels and eats it*)
Sophie Do you like bananas, Trev?
Trevor Yeah.
Brenda Do you want a bit?
Trevor No it's all right. I don't want to spoil my dinner.
Brenda Thank God for that.
Sophie I'd have got you one if I'd known. My mother bought six this
morning. You could have had mine.
Dilys (*off*) Are you staying for some dinner, Soph?
Sophie (*calling back*) What are you having?
Dilys (*off*) Beans and chips.
Sophie I should watch my figure.
Dilys (*off*) Well are you or not?
Sophie I'll just have a couple on a plate then.
Brenda (*with a mouthful of banana*) Oh . . . they're lovely.
Sophie (*after a pause*) Did you enjoy last night?
Trevor Yeah. It was a good night.
Sophie I enjoyed myself as well. (*A slight pause*) I enjoyed the walk home.
(*A slight pause*) It was a lovely night, wasn't it? (*A slight pause*) All the
stars were out and everything. (*A slight pause*) Do you remember walking
home?
Trevor I wasn't that drunk.
Sophie You weren't drunk, were you?
Trevor I'd had a few.
Sophie Oh that's it then. It was the drink talking.
Trevor What do you mean?
Sophie Does number seventeen Rotherham Street mean anything to you?
Trevor No, should it?
Sophie Well I just thought it might. We stopped outside there last night and
you asked me a question.
Trevor I didn't ask you to lend me money, did I? I've told you before,
always say no to me if I should ask.
Sophie No. It wasn't that. It wasn't money. (*A slight pause*) You asked me
to marry you.

Brenda stops chewing and counting

Trevor Oh that.
Sophie You did, didn't you?
Trevor Fancy remembering a joke like that.
Sophie (*after a slight pause*) A joke. (*She tries to laugh*) Yeah, that's right. I
said to Dilys it was a joke. (*She tries to laugh again as she sits on the arm of
the chair that all the pennies are on*)
Brenda (*with a mouthful of banana*) Now look what you've done.

Sophie springs to her feet. Brenda continues to grumble with her mouth full and Trevor and Sophie play their scene with their words running simultaneously with Brenda's

Brenda It's not fair. I'm going to have to count it all over again now. It'll take me ages. I was only half-way through it. I wish you'd look what you're doing, Sophie. If I lose any money down the side of the chair you'll just have to cover me that's all. It's a good job I didn't have my banana on there or you would have ruined it. I'd have made you buy me a whole pound just for myself.

Trevor Of course it wasn't a joke, silly.

Sophie It wasn't?

Trevor You don't think I'd joke about something like that.

Sophie I didn't know what to think, and I didn't like to say too much in case it all blew up in my face.

Trevor Well I meant it. Every word. All of it.

Sophie Oh Trev. (*She hugs him around the neck. She calls to Dilys*) It's all right. I didn't get it wrong after all, Dil. Oh I'm so happy I could—(*she shouts on the top of her voice*)—shout on the top of my voice.

Mother knocks from above

Dilys enters with Trevor's dinner

Dilys Has everybody gone mad?

Sophie We're getting married. I can't believe it. I can't believe it's happening to me.

Dilys Well put him down so's he can have his food, or you'll be marrying a seven-stone weakling.

Trevor (*sitting at the table*) Oh it smells lovely.

Dilys Are you hungry?

Trevor Hungry? (*He picks up his knife and fork*) I'm starving. I could eat a horse.

Brenda almost chokes on what's left of her banana. Dilys looks at her

Black-out

SCENE 2

The same. Late August, early evening

Sophie is standing on a dining-chair. The wireless is reporting the latest news from the front, and Brenda is in the kitchen

Sophie Come on, Brend. I don't want to be here all night.

Brenda (*off*) I'm just coming.

Sophie Trevor'll be ready before long and I don't want to keep him waiting.

Brenda enters with a little bowl with some liquid in it and a small cloth

Brenda Visiting isn't for another hour.

Sophie We're going to walk it. That will take us a good thirty minutes.
Brenda Right. Lift your skirt up.
Sophie (*tutting*) The times I've had that said to me.
Brenda What?
Sophie Nothing. It was a joke. Are you sure you can do it?
Brenda I watched Sandra do it for her sister last week it looked simple enough.
Sophie Just make sure it's nice and even. It's a dead give-away when a girl's got streaky legs. It's not too dark is it? You haven't got too much gravy browning?
Brenda It looks all right on my arm—look. (*She shows her arm to Sophie*)
Sophie You've got too much in there. Put that on my legs and from the waist down I'll look like Ella Fitzgerald.
Brenda It's all right honest. Are you ready? Here goes.

Brenda places the tiny rag into the watered gravy browning then to the top of Sophie's leg. Sophie jumps

What's the matter?
Sophie It's cold. The water's cold that's all. Try and make sure it looks natural.
Brenda How natural do you want it?
Sophie What do you mean?
Brenda Well if you like I'll draw you a nice little ladder just below your hem.
Sophie No, don't be soft. I'm going to the hospital. I can't go visiting with a ladder in my stocking. Where's the eyebrow pencil?
Brenda On the sideboard. (*She gets the eyebrow pencil from the sideboard and switches off the wireless*)
Sophie I reckon that'll be the hardest bit. Getting the seams straight.
Brenda (*after a pause*) How much longer do you think Mammy will be in hospital?
Sophie (*after a slight pause*) Oh I don't know. I suppose she'll be there a bit yet.
Brenda They think I don't know.
Sophie (*after a slight pause*) Who?
Brenda Trevor and Dilys.
Sophie About what?
Brenda Mammy.
Sophie What about her?
Brenda She's not going to get better, is she?
Sophie Who said that?
Brenda Nobody, I just know.
Sophie Don't be silly.
Brenda You know too, don't you, Soph?
Sophie Come on hurry up and start the other leg. I've got to go.
Brenda (*after a slight pause, then resuming*) She nearly told me the night they took her into hospital.
Sophie What did she say?
Brenda Nothing. She just looked at me.

Sophie It's all in your mind. In a couple of weeks she'll be up and about and jumping over your head. You wait and see. How is it looking?

Brenda All right. I can't see any streaks yet.

Sophie Good.

Brenda (*after a slight pause*) Do you think I should tell Dilys?

She doesn't answer

That I know?

Sophie (*after a slight pause*) No.

Brenda Why?

Sophie Because I think keeping it from you is all that's keeping Dilys together. You show her that you know and she won't be able to cope. You won't say anything, will you?

Brenda Course I won't. I just thought I should say something because people think I'm a little girl. I'm not anymore, you know. I'm a woman now. I wear a belt.

Sophie A what?

Brenda A belt. You know. Once a month.

Sophie Oh I see. (*Embarrassed*) Come on start the other leg.

Brenda I haven't half done this one yet. Do you know what, Soph?

Sophie What?

Brenda You've got awful hairy legs for a woman.

Sophie (*after a slight pause*) I don't think you'd better say anything to Trevor either. About your mother.

Brenda All right.

Sophie It hasn't been easy for him as well as Dilys. He's very sensitive too. Oh I know he doesn't show it—but that's just his outside. His shell. I'm making him sound like a cockle.

Brenda Have you noticed Dilys isn't looking very well lately?

Sophie Between everything I'm not surprised.

Brenda She always seems as if she's just been crying.

Sophie She's under a lot of strain. And of course there's Greg.

Brenda I wish he hadn't gone away. Although I don't know, if he hadn't I wouldn't have had all that money.

Sophie How much was it?

Brenda Five pounds, two shillings and eleven pence.

Sophie As much as that?

Brenda Yeah. If I let you into a secret will you promise not to tell Trevor?

Sophie Go on then.

Brenda There was only three pounds there really. I told him it was five because he said he'd double it.

Sophie (*laughing*) Shall I let you into a secret?

Brenda nods as she laughs

He knew.

Brenda Oh I wish you hadn't told me. It was much more fun thinking I'd got away with it.

Sophie How's it coming?

Brenda I think I'm ready for the pencil now.

Sophie Be careful and take your time. Go back to the first leg. Give this one time to dry.

Brenda Keep still now then, right?

She begins to draw the line and Sophie giggles

What's the matter?

Sophie It tickles.

There is a pause in which Brenda continues to draw the line on Sophie's leg

Brenda Before Mammy went into hospital and me and Dilys shared the bedroom I used to hear her cry a lot. She used to wake me up sometimes. If I'd called her though she'd never answer. She'd stop but she'd never answer. If that's what being in love is like I hope it never happens to me.

Sophie It's not always like that, being upset is only part of it.

Brenda I think I'll be a nun. There we are, how's that?

Sophie Have you done them straight?

Brenda They look all right.

Sophie (*getting down off the chair*) I still feel a bit tacky.

Brenda Go and stand by the fire then.

Sophie stands with her back to where the fire is placed. She raises her skirt in order to dry her legs

Brenda takes the little bowl of gravy-water and the rag out to the kitchen

Trevor enters from upstairs

Sophie (*to Trevor*) I'm just about ready.

Trevor What are you doing?

Sophie Drying my legs. (*She shows him*) Well ... what do you think?

Trevor About what?

Sophie My legs.

Trevor (*after looking at them*) They're all right. A bit short and stumpy, but as legs go they're not bad. Have you seen my mother's old brown handbag?

Sophie I didn't know your mother had an old brown handbag.

Trevor She doesn't use it. She just keeps things in it.

Brenda enters

Sophie You'd better ask Dilys. I wouldn't know where to look for it. Or ask Brenda, perhaps she'd know.

Brenda What?

Sophie Where your mother keeps her old brown handbag.

Brenda There's a black one in the sideboard.

Trevor Brown, Brend, I've got to find her brown one.

Brenda Ask Dilys.

Sophie That's what I said. (*To Trevor*) Don't ask her now though, she's sleeping.

Trevor No she's not. She's coming down.

Brenda What does Mammy want her old handbag for?

Trevor doesn't answer. He shrugs his shoulders and looks at Sophie

Sophie I expect there's things in there she wants. (*To Trevor*) Didn't she tell you where it was?

Trevor She couldn't remember.

Brenda Come on, Trev, let's empty the sideboard.

Sophie Better leave it till Dilys comes down. She might be able to put her hands on it straightaway.

Brenda proceeds to empty the sideboard regardless

(*To Trevor*) I hope she starts pulling herself together.

He looks at her

Dilys.

Trevor It's not an easy thing to accept.

Sophie It's not just your mother.

Trevor No I know. That Yank's upsetting her as well.

Sophie Has she said anything?

Trevor No—nothing. What about you?

Sophie Not a word. Well . . . nothing we don't already know. Which isn't very much.

Trevor If I could get my hands on him I'd bloody kill him. They were nothing but trouble from the day they got here.

Dilys enters

Dily's Who?

Sophie (*after a slight pause*) We're looking for your mother's brown handbag.

Trevor She asked me to take it in for her.

Dilys There's one in her wardrobe.

Brenda leaves the sideboard and is about to leave the room

On the middle shelf. I don't remember the colour. (*To Brenda*) Where are you going?

Brenda To fetch it.

Brenda exits

Trevor (*calling after her*) Don't you look inside it, mind.

Dilys looks at him

She asked me not to.

There is an awkward pause

Shall I put the kettle on?

Dilys doesn't answer

Right. I'll go and put the kettle on.

He exits to the kitchen

Sophie Look at this mess. Brenda's left everything out. (*She begins to put everything back into the sideboard*)
Dilys (*after a slight pause*) Is there coal in the bucket?
Sophie Do you want Trevor to put some on?
Dilys No I'll do it later. I just wanted to make sure there was some cracked, that's all.
Sophie Why don't you come with us to the hospital?
Dilys No I can't go tonight again. I need a night in.

At this point Sophie finds a letter. She stands to look at it. She slowly moves towards Dilys

Sophie Hey Dil, look what I found.
Dilys What are you doing with that?
Sophie I found it in the sideboard. You've forgotten to post it.
Dilys Give it to me. (*She takes the letter and puts it back in the sideboard*)
Sophie Well don't put it back in there, you'll forget it again.
Dilys No I won't.
Sophie Why don't you give it to me? I'll post it on my way to the hospital.
Dilys It's all right.
Sophie Aren't you going to post it, Dil?

Dilys doesn't answer

It's going to Greg's wife, isn't it?

Dilys doesn't answer

What do you want to write to her for?
Dilys I didn't write it. Greg did.
Sophie Why didn't he post it then?
Dilys It's telling his wife it's finished between them. He wanted me to post it to make the decision.
Sophie You don't want him to finish with his wife, do you?
Dilys I never said that.
Sophie It's a fair assumption, Dil. Greg's been gone a month and the letter's still in the sideboard.
Dilys I've wanted to post it. Three times I put my coat on to go down to the post office, and three times I took it off.
Sophie Don't you love him?
Dilys (*frustrated*) Yes.
Sophie Does he love you?
Dilys Yes.
Sophie Has he told you?
Dilys Yes.
Sophie Do you believe him?
Dilys Why shouldn't I?
Sophie Men say they love you all the time, but it doesn't mean anything.
Dilys Greg means it.
Sophie What's the problem then? If he loves you post it.

Dilys It's not as easy as that.
Sophie What's difficult about it?
Dilys You don't understand. (*After a slight pause*) Do you love Trevor?
Sophie Yeah.
Dilys Does he love you?
Sophie Of course he does.
Dilys Has he told you?

Sophie is about to say yes, then decides to say the truth

Sophie No. (*She retorts*) He doesn't say things like that, Trevor does things.
Dilys Like what?
Sophie (*searching for an answer then replying*) Trevor posts his own letters.
Dilys (*after a slight pause*) So you love him?
Sophie I'm marrying him, aren't I?
Dilys But why are you getting married?
Sophie (*after a slight pause*) Because I'm twenty-eight.
Dilys Is it going to be enough for you having Trevor?
Sophie Of course it is.
Dilys Don't you want something more?
Sophie Yeah. I want a house of our own—nice things—his kids.
Dilys Is that all?
Sophie What else is there?
Dilys There's got to be more to life than a house, a husband and children.
Sophie There is.
Dilys Tell me then. Tell me what it is.
Sophie Grandchildren, stupid. What more do you want than that?
Dilys I don't know what I want anymore. I just want something else.
Sophie Do me a favour then, will you? Don't spend too long looking for it or you'll be fifty before you realize it's not there. It doesn't exist—and never has. You'll be like that dog of yours. He spends half his life chasing his tail—and where has he got? Nowhere. All he ever does is go round in circles.
Trevor (*off, from the kitchen*) I can't find the tea.
Sophie It's in the caddy on the window sill. (*After a pause*) What are you doing to do, Dil? You've got to sort yourself out. You can't go on like this.
Dilys Listen to you. Have you heard yourself? You're trying to give me advice.
Sophie I'm trying to help you that's all.
Dilys You! Four months ago I brought you home to meet Trevor because you couldn't pick up with anyone. I felt sorry for you. And now here you are telling me what to do.
Sophie (*hurt*) I didn't know you brought me home because you felt sorry for me.
Dilys Well you know now.
Sophie I thought it was because Trevor liked me.
Dilys (*after a pause*) Oh I'm sorry, Soph. I didn't mean that. (*She sighs heavily*) Oh I don't know. It's all right for you. You don't know how

lucky you are. I don't even know where Greg is. At least you know where
Trevor is.

There is the sound of an almighty crash from the kitchen, saucepans, etc.

Sophie Yeah, he's in the kitchen.

They laugh

That night you brought me back here I thought you'd dropped me right
in it.

Dilys What did you tell him? (*Before Sophie can answer she continues*) It
doesn't matter now, does it? When are you getting married?

Sophie Soon. Soon I expect. We haven't set a date yet, but it won't be long.

Dilys Are you sure it's what you want?

Sophie Yeah. What do you want?

Brenda rushes in with a brown handbag

Brenda I found it. (*She gives the bag to Dilys*)

Trevor (*off, from the kitchen*) Sophie! Come and give me a hand, will you?
I'm in one hell of a mess.

Sophie exits to the kitchen

Brenda Is that the right one?

Dilys I don't know. I expect so.

Brenda (*after a slight pause*) Are you all right, Dil?

Dilys nods

Have you heard from Greg?

Dilys Not yet.

Brenda Is he coming back do you think?

Dilys I don't know.

Brenda Do you want him to?

Dilys Oh shut up, Brenda. For goodness sake shut up.

Brenda storms off upstairs

Brenda! (*She stands there for a moment. She is mixed up and annoyed with
herself. She turns back into the room and makes some frustrated gesture
with her fists. She looks at the handbag, goes to it and opens it. She takes out
a few things, then a photograph. She looks at it then takes out some letters.
She opens one and reads it*)

Trevor enters

*As Dilys turns over the page to read what is written on the other side, she
becomes aware of Trevor's presence. She looks up*

Do you know what she keeps?

Trevor What are you doing?

Dilys There's letters. She's been keeping letters from——

Trevor You shouldn't be looking in there.

Dilys She had a friend—a boyfriend.

Trevor I know.
Dilys There's a photograph too.
Trevor I know. (*He crosses to her and replaces everything in the handbag*)

He then leaves the room

Dilys is left dumbfounded

Black-out

SCENE 3

The same. September, evening

Mother is on the settee, Trevor is in the armchair reading. Sophie and Dilys are cutting out Sophie's wedding outfit on the floor. The wireless is on

Mother It's your Aunty Mavis had the biggest wedding I'd ever seen. Well it wasn't so much big—I mean there wasn't that much to eat—a cup of tea and two sandwiches as I remember—but the whole village turned out for it. She had a beautiful day even though I spent most of it in the kitchen. Somebody had to wash all those dishes. I don't think I'd ever seen so many, and by the end of the day I didn't care if I'd never see another cup as long as I lived.

The others all react to this remark

I had a lovely dress for it. My mother made it special. She was marvellous with her hands.
Sophie Careful now, Dilys. If you make a mistake cutting out, I'll have to get married in my clippy uniform.
Dilys I've cut out before.
Sophie Yeah I know. Remember that pin cushion you made? It started out as a pillow case.
Dilys Out the way, Trevor. Move your foot. No hang on. Make yourself useful. (*She takes his foot and places it in the middle of the pattern*)
Sophie I wish I was able to buy something new. I'm afraid to think what this is going to turn out like.
Dilys It'll be very smart. You wait and see. We've got some lace. That'll tart it up a bit.
Sophie I'm not sure about it myself.
Dilys You're going to look lovely, don't panic.
Sophie (*holding the lace to her chest*) I'm not a lacy person.
Dilys You need a bit of lace on the chest to break it up a bit. What do you say, Mam? (*To Sophie*) Show her.

Sophie does

Mother Yes, but you don't want it all the way down there though. It just needs a bit around the neck.
Sophie What do you think, Trev?

Trevor About what?
Sophie The lace. Should I just have a bit up here or what? (*She puts a little bit of lace around her neck*)
Trevor Oh I don't know, Soph. I don't know what to say.

Sophie goes to look in the mirror

Dilys I think it should be more on the bodice.
Sophie (*after looking in the mirror*) Oh and me. I can't wear it like this. It looks like a dog's collar.
Trevor How long do you reckon you'll be, Soph?
Sophie Why?
Trevor Well I thought we'd nip out and have a drink.
Sophie Oh I won't be ready for a bit yet. We've got to pin it all together and everything. Haven't we, Dil?
Voice from wireless We interrupt this programme with an important news item. The armed might of America's army, navy, coastguards and thousands of local police was suddenly mobilized today as guard for the nation's principle defence establishments, when rumours of a nationwide plot were heard in Washington. Word received by intelligence services hinted that zero hour for sabotage at America's most vital war plants and shipping centres would come during this weekend. Ships, piers, warehouses and harbour facilities at all principal ports are under close watch.
Trevor (*during this*) Sshhh! There's a newsflash.
Sophie What?
Trevor A newsflash.
Dilys Sshhh.
Trevor Don't tell me to shush, Dilys.
Dilys Look, shut up, Trevor.
Trevor All right then, I'll shut up.
Sophie Don't make such a noise, Trevor.
Trevor Shut up, Soph.

There is a pause while they all listen for a moment, then Trevor switches off the wireless

Mother Where's it all going to end?
Sophie My mother says we're not half-way through it yet.
Mother I've got an awful feeling she's right.
Trevor Have you finished with my foot, Dil?
Dilys Pass me some pins, Soph.   ﹐
Sophie (*doing so*) Trev, are you going to have a new shirt?
Trevor Yeah, I might, yeah.
Sophie How many coupons have you got?
Trevor I don't know, I haven't counted them yet.
Sophie Well hurry up and count them then. We haven't got long.

Suddenly the Lights go out

Mother Oh the shilling's gone.
Sophie Don't move anyone.

Trevor I'll go and put one in.
Sophie Stay where you are, Trevor.
Trevor I'm going to put a shilling in the meter.
Sophie No, you'll walk on my dress.
Trevor No I won't.
Mother There should be a shilling under the runner.
Brenda (*off*) Mammy!
Dilys I'll get it.
Sophie Don't come this way.
Dilys It'll be all right. (*She goes towards the hall*)
Sophie Watch my dress everyone.
Brenda (*off*) Mammy!
Mother There's Brenda now. What are you doing down here?
Brenda (*off*) I couldn't see, could I.
Sophie Well, don't come in here you'll stand on my dress.

Brenda enters

Brenda I was reading and the lights went out.
Mother What are you doing reading at this time of night? You've got
school in the morning. Back to bed.
Trevor Come on, I'll show you up.
Sophie Careful, Trevor.

Trevor takes Brenda to the stairs

Brenda exits

Dilys There's not one here, Mam, we must have run out.
Mother Are you sure?
Dilys (*coming back into the room*) There's nothing under the runner at all.
Mother It's pointless looking for my purse, I know I haven't got one. What
about you, Trevor? Have you got any shilling pieces?
Trevor No only coppers I've got.
Mother Sophie?
Sophie I left my purse in the house.
Dilys I gave the only one I had to you yesterday.
Mother Somebody'll have to go and find some then.
Trevor I'll go. Do you want to come with me, Soph?
Sophie Yes all right.
Mother Try not to be too long, Trevor.
Trevor Back in five minutes.

*He leaves the room with Sophie, but she is unaware that she has caught her
shoe in the material. When she leaves the room she drags the remains of her
unfinished dress behind her*

Mother Find the torch, Dilys. We've got candles here too, haven't we? They
should be in the sideboard drawer.

Dilys finds the torch and switches it on. She then looks for candles

Dilys We're always being caught out like this.

Mother I thought sure I put a shilling under there this morning.

Dilys You couldn't have or it would be there now.

Dilys takes one candle and goes out to the kitchen. There is a slight pause

Mother I used to sit for hours like this when I was a girl. It was all oil lamps then. (*A slight pause*) I remember the first time they came to put electric in my mother's house. We couldn't believe it. We all thought it was marvellous. A miracle. (*A slight pause*) We take everything too much for granted these days. (*Reflecting again*) There was a time when if you had electric light you were well off.

Dilys enters with a lighted candle. She puts it down on the table, switches off the torch and puts that down on the sideboard

Dilys Is that all right?

Mother It'll do till Trevor comes.

Dilys God knows how long he'll be. They'll probably end up in the pub. (*A slight pause*) Why don't you go up to bed?

Mother He'll be all right with Sophie, won't he?

Dilys Oh yes. I wouldn't worry about Trevor.

Mother I only hope I'll be here to see him married.

Dilys Of course you will, Mam.

Mother I know what it means when they look at you in hospital stitch you up quick and send you home. Nothing to be done. Best to accept it. And I have. It's just you children I'm worried about.

Dilys I'll be all right.

Mother You're not happy, are you?

Dilys Who is.

Mother It's that boy, isn't it? That American.

Dilys doesn't answer

He hasn't left you with anything, has he?

Dilys What do you mean?

Mother A baby.

Dilys Oh Mam.

Mother (*after a slight pause*) Have you heard from him?

Dilys No.

Mother (*sighing*) I told you what would happen. They're all the same. Better put him out of your mind.

Dilys I'm not sure I can do that.

Mother You must make yourself.

Dilys You can talk.

Mother What do you mean?

Dilys It's not easy, is it? You know, Mam. Yes you do.

Mother (*after a slight pause*) There was a time when I was a bit like you wanting something I couldn't have.

Dilys Wanting something different?

Mother (*almost to herself*) Someone different. (*After a slight pause*) I had a friend you know, before I married your father. His name was Philip.

Dilys I know.

Mother (*after a slight pause*) I loved him.

Dilys I know. I saw the letters. I'm sorry.

Mother It was better to settle for what I could get. I haven't had much in life—but at least I've had you kids . . . (*She silently breaks down*)

Dilys (*kneeling beside her*) I know, I know.

Mother Do you remember what your father used to say to you? He was almost right, but sometimes it's better to grab something even if it doesn't make you happy. You'll find something that's good in it. Maybe you never really learn to leave go, but it's nice to have something to hang on to sometimes.

Dilys Don't you think it might have been easier if you destroyed them?

Mother (*after a slight pause*) I don't know. I don't know.

Dilys (*after a pause*) Did you love Daddy?

Mother Yes, I loved him . . . but it wasn't what it should have been. I settled for what I could get and not for what I needed.

Dilys I'm not sure you settled for anything.

Mother I don't regret what I did.

Dilys Don't you?

Mother How can I? When I look at my kids, how can I? (*A slight pause*) You'll take care of Brenda, won't you? She'll be all right?

Dilys Of course she will.

Mother I know it's not going to be easy for you, but try and be happy? For me? Try taking a page out of Sophie's book.

Dilys Mam, I don't want to be like Sophie.

Mother She's a happy girl.

Dilys Sophie's only happy because Trevor makes her happy.

Mother What's wrong with that?

Dilys What if something happens to Trevor?

Mother Don't talk like that.

Dilys Sophie'd never make it on her own. I don't want to be like that. I want to be happy because of me. (*She thinks about what she has just said*)

Mother You're a funny girl, Dilys. But you're a good girl. (*After a slight pause*) I think I'll go up now.

Dilys Take the torch.

Mother All right.

Dilys Do you want a hot drink?

Mother No, I won't bother.

Dilys I'll see you in the morning then.

Mother It's funny really. I didn't know whether to ask you to take care of Brenda, or Brenda to take care of you.

Dilys I'm going to be all right, Mam.

Mother Are you?

Dilys I'm going to make myself. Love isn't hanging on, Mam. It's letting go.

Mother (*turning to go*) Yes. There's nothing better than your family, really.

Mother exits with the torch

Dilys watches her ascend the stairs. After a moment she turns into the room. She goes to the sideboard and takes out the letter. She moves to the candlelight and is about to open the letter when she changes her mind. She looks at it for a second before she burns it on the candle. After she has done this . . .

    Brenda enters

Brenda Dil?
Dilys What are you doing back up?
Brenda I couldn't sleep.
Dilys Come and sit down till Trevor comes.

They both sit on the settee

Brenda Will he be long?
Dilys I don't know . . . Why?
Brenda Dil, are you afraid of anything?
Dilys I suppose everybody is afraid of something.
Brenda What are you afraid of?
Dilys I'm exceptional. I'm not afraid of anything.
Brenda Nothing at all.
Dilys No, not anymore.
Brenda (*after a slight pause*) I'm afraid of the dark.
Dilys You're not.
Brenda I am, I hate it.
Dilys There's nothing to be afraid of, Brenda.
Brenda Hold me, Dil.

Dilys does

    Tighter.

Trevor and Sophie are heard out in the passage

Sophie (*off*) What are you doing, Trevor? No, don't be silly—they'll hear us. (*She laughs*) Stop it. (*She laughs again*) Trevor.
Brenda Is that you, Trev?
Trevor (*off*) Shit!
Sophie (*off*) Yeah, we're just putting the shilling in. I can't reach, Trevor. Pass me a chair. No, don't pick me up. No, put me down.
Trevor (*off*) Can you reach it?

Sophie puts the coin in the meter and the light comes on. All we see of Sophie from the hallway is from her knees down

Seconds after the Lights come on, a man's voice is heard from outside the house

Voice (*off*) Oy! Turn that bloody light out!

                  CURTAIN

FURNITURE AND PROPERTY LIST

ACT I

SCENE 1

On stage: Settee. *On it:* newspaper under cushion
Armchair
Sideboard. *On it:* wireless, photographs, handbag with compact
  inside. *In drawer:* orange papers. *Inside:* dressing
Mirror on wall
Table. *On it:* sugar-bowl, milk jug, tablecloth
Chairs
Fireplace with coal fire effect. *By it:* bucket of coal
Carpet
Window curtains (open)
Curtain over door to passage
Coat hooks in passage
Meter in hall above living-room door
Shilling under runner in passage

Off stage: Parcel of chips **(Mother)**
3 plates, cutlery, salt, vinegar **(Brenda)**
Loaf of bread, bread knife **(Dilys)**
Pot of tea **(Brenda)**
4 cups and saucers **(Brenda)**
Towel **(Mother)**
2 coats **(Dilys)**
Chips **(Mother)**
Cup of water **(Brenda)**

Personal: **Dilys:** wrist-watch

SCENE 2

Strike: **Dilys's** handbag and coat
Bread, knife, teapot, any other dishes from table
Towel

Re-set: Window curtains open

Set: Money in purse in sideboard drawer

Off stage: Parcel of meat, money, ration book **(Brenda)**
2 cups and saucers **(Dilys)**
Potatoes, bread **(Brenda)**

Personal: **Greg:** bar of chocolate in pocket

ACT II

SCENE 1

Strike: Potatoes, bread
Cups, saucers
Purse, money

Set: Potatoes, paper, knife, bowl on table
Banana for **Brenda**

Off stage: Tea-tin full of pennies, stamp **(Brenda)**
Tin-bath **(Sophie)**
Dinner on plate, knife, fork **(Dilys)**

Personal: **Greg:** letter in inside pocket

SCENE 2

Strike: Plate, cutlery, tea-tin, pennies

Set: Eyebrow pencil on sideboard
Black handbag inside sideboard

Off stage: Small bowl of brown liquid, rag **(Brenda)**
Brown handbag containing letters, photograph **(Brenda)**

SCENE 3

Strike: Handbag

Set: Paper/book for **Trevor**
Material, pattern, lace, pins, scissors, etc. on floor
Torch (practical) on sideboard
Candles in sideboard drawer

Off stage: Lighted candle **(Dilys)**

LIGHTING PLOT

Practical fittings required: coal fire effect, pendant in living-room, lights in passage and kitchen

Interior. A living-room. The same scene throughout

ACT I SCENE 1 Late evening

To open: Darkness, apart from orange glow from fire

Cue 1	**Sophie** puts coin in meter *Snap up interior lighting, pendant on*	(Page 1)
Cue 2	**Brenda** goes to kitchen, smiling smugly at **Sophie** and switches on kitchen light *Snap up light in kitchen*	(Page 2)
Cue 3	**Dilys** goes to kitchen and switches off light *Snap off kitchen light*	(Page 18)
Cue 4	**Dilys** switches off living-room light *Snap off pendant, leaving orange glow from dying fire*	(Page 18)

ACT II SCENE 2 Afternoon

To open: General interior lighting, fire effect on

Cue 5	**Mother** looks at **Dilys** and they both laugh *Fade to black-out*	(Page 29)

ACT II SCENE 1 Afternoon

To open: General interior lighting, fire effect on

Cue 6	**Brenda** almost chokes on her banana. **Dilys** looks at her *Black-out*	(Page 41)

ACT II SCENE 2 Early evening

To open: General interior lighting, fire effect on

Cue 7	**Trevor** goes out of the room, leaving **Dilys** dumbfounded *Black-out*	(Page 49)

ACT II SCENE 3   Evening

To open: General interior lighting, pendant on, fire effect on

Cue 8   **Sophie:** "We haven't got long."   (Page 50)
          Black-out, apart from fire effect

Cue 9   As **Dilys** enters with lighted candle   (Page 52)
          Increase lighting slightly

Cue 10 **Sophie** puts coin in meter   (Page 54)
          Snap up general lighting, pendant on, passage light on

EFFECTS PLOT

ACT I

Cue 1	Shortly after CURTAIN rises *Front door opens and closes*	(Page 1)
Cue 2	**Dilys:** "You look lovely." *Front door opens and slams*	(Page 4)
Cue 3	**Mother** exits to kitchen *Back door opens and slams*	(Page 4)
Cue 4	**Dilys** puts compact back in her bag *Back door opens and slams*	(Page 8)
Cue 5	**Sophie:** "... put him out or anything." No-one answers *Front door opens and slams*	(Page 9)
Cue 6	**Brenda:** "... if he hasn't asked you." *Knock from above*	(Page 16)
Cue 7	**Greg** kisses **Dilys** *Front door opens and slams*	(Page 20)
Cue 8	**Dilys:** "If you mess this up for me ..." *Front door opens and slams*	(Page 24)
Cue 9	**Dilys:** "... another Yank at all." *Sound of kettle boiling from kitchen*	(Page 25)
Cue 10	**Dilys** exits to kitchen *Cut kettle sound*	(Page 25)
Cue 11	**Mother:** "... in my bedroom then." *Front door opens and slams*	(Page 26)

ACT II

Cue 12	**Brenda:** "... keep it till tomorrow." *Knock at front door*	(Page 30)
Cue 13	**Brenda** leaves to answer front door *Front door opens and closes*	(Page 30)
Cue 14	**Greg:** "... have to go. Now." They look at each other *Front door opens and slams*	(Page 32)
Cue 15	**Sophie:** "That steak smells lovely" *Front door opens and slams*	(Page 35)
Cue 16	**Dilys:** "Give the chips a shake, Brend." *Front door opens and slams*	(Page 37)

MADE AND PRINTED IN GREAT BRITAIN BY
LATIMER TREND & COMPANY LTD PLYMOUTH

MADE IN ENGLAND